PhB
the

PROFESSIONAL HUMAN BEING

Profiting from Purpose

John M. Bean

To Peter Brosius —
Consider this book part of
your continuing education credits.
You passed the qualifying course
long ago!

Warmest regards,

John Bean

Beaver's Pond Press, Inc.
Edina, Minnesota

ISBN 1-59298-086-4

Library of Congress Catalog Number: 2004097963

Book design and typesetting: Mori Studio
Cover design: Mori Studio

Printed in the United States of America

First Printing: November 2004

07 06 05 04   6 5 4 3 2 1

Beaver's Pond Press, Inc.   7104 Ohms Lane, Suite 216
Edina, MN 55439
(952) 829-8818
www.BeaversPondPress.com

To order, visit www.BookHouseFulfillment.com or call 1-800-901-3480. Reseller and special sales discounts available.

DEDICATION

This book is dedicated to all of us—human beings that are
Needy
Greedy
Warm
Wonderful
Inefficient
Indispensable

To our strengths and weaknesses,
our creativity and our uniqueness.

May each of us find our purpose
and fulfillment in this world!

TABLE
OF CONTENTS

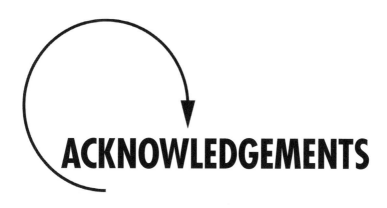

ACKNOWLEDGEMENTS

First, as always, Babette.

Being married to a writer is not an easy role to play. You see, when a writer is looking out the window, drumming fingers, exercising, or doing almost anything else that seems like a useless task, he or she is really working—sometimes with great effort. It just doesn't seem like work to the observer. Thank you for putting up with all my quirks and shenanigans.

Thanks to my family—son and daughter and spouses and grandchildren, father, mother, brothers, and sisters. First, you shaped me. Then you encouraged me.

Thanks to my friends who also shaped and encouraged me.

Thanks to Bruce, Theresa, Dave, Mary Jo, and Steve—my PhBs—who allowed me to share their stories with you as they had shared them with me.

Thanks to Carolyn Gable of New Age Transportation. She is a dynamo!

Thanks to Carol Turner who helped me screw up the courage to go for it. Yes, Carol, the universe will answer you back when you state your intentions.

Thanks to Milt Adams of Beaver's Pond Press. A most generous soul, Milt provided sage advice and was my guide through the brand-new landscape of book publishing.

Thanks to Stephen Collins who took the time not only to read but to edit my manuscript while in the midst of production of his television show, *Seventh Heaven.*

Thanks to Nancy Franke Wilson and Wendy Robson (Magic Wendy) for their energy, creativity, and public relations skills.

Thanks to Kian Dwyer, a fellow author (*Living Your Chosen Eulogy: Choosing to Live Your Most Honorable Self*), who kept me persistent and helped me progress every day.

Thanks to Chuck Parten, the first personal coach I ever met and who inspired me to take a new, exciting direction in my life.

Thanks to Steve Moore who always encouraged me to write, acted as an editor and advisor, and expanded my spiritual horizons as few others have.

Finally, thanks to that great and grand power that is above us all. You can't do this kind of thing all alone, you know.

STEPPING UP

Business is not Personal

*T*he year was 1975, and I was on my first major call for the United Way.

I had been included in the retinue that was calling on a very large corporate donor. The four of us walked into the executive's office, one after the other—the general campaign chairman, his aide-de-camp, the head campaign director, and me.

The general campaign chairman was the CEO of the local telephone company (in those days Ma Bell ruled the land). He smiled widely as he extended his hand in a friendly hello.

"Sam, how are you?" he said warmly. "It's so good of you to give us the time for this call. How are Mary and the children?"

Thus began a 30-minute meeting to ask this business leader to support the upcoming United Way campaign both personally and corporately. Our campaign chairman spoke eloquently of our human obligation to one another and how instrumental the United Way was in helping all humankind in our community. He also smiled and professed great interest in every aspect of the prospective donor's business and personal life. He really buttered him up.

Of course, the campaign chairman really didn't know the prospect from a hole in the ground. Most of the information he used had been researched by the United Way staff. But you would have thought that he and Sam were really just best buddies who hadn't met yet.

When we had concluded the call and departed, the warm, wide smile disappeared suddenly and completely. In its place was a blank mask.

"Analysis!" he snapped in the direction of his trusty aide.

His aide gave a very detailed description of what had happened including body language, dress, and visual cues. He concluded that he thought the prospect CEO would "stand up and salute," but he couldn't be sure.

"We'd better find out who his largest customer is in case we have to 'persuade' this guy. By God, I am going to make our goal no matter what!"

The only sound after that was the milk of humanity evaporating from our group.

This is a short course about becoming human. I've called it PhB—Professional Human Being—to indicate, in a whimsical way perhaps—both the seriousness and the latent dignity of the undertaking. I welcome you to give it a try.

There's an old saying from the South: "I gotta feelin' we've run past more than we'll ever catch up to." This is your chance to back up a bit so you can go forward a lot.

The basic underlying question that has been gnawing at me for years is:

Why is it that many people who are rational, compassionate, and caring when you meet them in almost any other social situation, become cold, calculating, unfeeling, and sometimes bizarrely irrational as soon as they walk through the door at work?

I'm well aware that work life is usually not quite the same as other facets of our lives. All the same, when I hear the standard line that "this is business, not personal," I find myself wondering...

Isn't everything we do personal?

If we succeed in shutting down that personal part of ourselves completely during the hours we're at work—which is cumulatively almost half our lives—aren't we in danger of losing the ability to restart our personal selves once we've left the office?

These questions were on my mind when I began to write this book.

In the course of working out these themes on paper, I came to several simple but valuable realizations. On the plus side:

- I discovered that I really like people.

  Unlike Will Rogers, I *have* met a few people I didn't like, but not many. And quite often I discovered later that the unlikable person was in some kind of distress. I claim to really dislike only two or three of the thousands of people I have met in my life.

- I learned the importance of really listening to people. I stilled my ego, resisted the temptation to form judgments prematurely, and listened to what others had to say. As a result, I have been repeatedly delighted and amazed to discover far more about what others are thinking and how they're feeling than I would have otherwise. Learning to plumb the depths of a person's soul rewards you with a realization of how different we all *are and how positively unique each of us is.*

- The wonder of it all.

  Almost everyone I have met has something deep inside them that needs fulfillment, a void that needs to be filled.

For some it's money and power, but for most it's something larger than they are.

My efforts to probe this longing for a larger fulfillment lie at the heart of this book. It is also why I became a personal coach.

On the negative side, I also became painfully aware of the joylessness many people feel at work.

- I have worked for many organizations and studied numerous others. I was in the investment business for 27 years.

  I once read a study concluding that 80 percent of the employees in the United States would quit their jobs tomorrow if they could. Why? For most of them, money wasn't the issue. Rather, they longed to find work that was more meaningful, to be treated like a human being, to be sincerely praised, to be truly appreciated, and to be given the opportunity to perform meaningful tasks.

- Ego and greed.

  I don't mean to pick on corporate America because they represent only a portion of the ego and greed disease. It's just that those few executives who give all the others a bad name really know how to mess things up!

  If a celebrity does something illegal or outrageous, it usually affects very few people, even though we all hear about it. When the executive does something illegal or outrageous, we seldom hear about it, although in many cases the results are catastrophic, with *many* people suffering low morale, the loss of jobs, and even financial ruin.

  Many such business fiascos are the result of the oldest of maladies—ego and greed.

- Intolerance.

  Politics has become a partisan quagmire of hate and destruction. It is not enough to simply disagree. It seems we must denigrate our opponents and attempt to destroy the opposition no matter which side of the aisle or the issue.

We sue each other at the drop of a hat. The courts become the first resort instead of the last.

And everyone has their issue that they will defend to the death—preferably yours, not theirs.

Cause

I don't pretend to know how we have come to this pass of cynicism and intolerance, but I do have a few guesses.

* The unexamined life.

Socrates observed, "The unexamined life is not worth living."

The 24/7 culture that has evolved leaves us precious little time to examine our lives. We seem to career from one task, project, assignment, or crisis to another. Or we're always doing "something for the kids." Often that means acting as chauffeurs on the way to the too many activities we've signed them up for.

Examining life is not easy. It takes time. Yet it seems to me it is an essential exercise for discovering and plotting meaningful direction for ourselves. When we take the time to examine life, both as individuals and as organizations, we are more likely to discover *a higher purpose.*

* Lack of a higher purpose.

For many people and organizations, profit is their sole motivation for work.

These days it seems as if the old saying, "He who dies with the most toys wins" (a phrase that was conceived as a mirthful observation) has become an actual goal to be achieved!

Make no mistake about it. People have the right to earn what they can at whatever endeavor they choose. Certainly if organizations do not make profits, they will cease to exist. It's OK to earn money and make profits. But when earning the money and making profits become the *only* goals, the world becomes shallow and petty. When our thoughts are consumed with "making the numbers" rather than all the things *behind* making the numbers, we begin to think primarily of ourselves and our numbers, not the greater good, the higher purpose, or something bigger than we are.

History

Postwar affluence and expanding access to higher education made the 1960s a period of liberation in American society. In recent times the Internet has further carried that liberation throughout the world. Although it's clear that tyranny still holds sway in many parts of the world, nevertheless no period in history has seen so much freedom around the globe. Nations can no longer control the flow of information that reaches their citizens. CNN and the Internet have stripped away the shroud of censorship. Now we can communicate with anyone anywhere and ask them directly, "What's going on with you?"

There was another side to the '60s, however, which has given us a more troubling legacy—I refer to the mantra, "Do Your Own Thing."

In the 1950s, everyone was trying to do the *same* thing. Certain things were not spoken of, and being different was generally frowned upon. Etiquette and manners seemed to be laws unto themselves, not to be broken no matter how silly they appeared to be.

Wham! Bam! Along came the '60s. "Do your own thing" was the liberating concept.

Forget the rules! Do your own thing!

Etiquette? Manners? These are the marks of an uptight, neurotic society, rife with decay and about to collapse. Get down! Do your own thing!

Indeed, this *was* liberating. Blowing up the old stereotypes resulted in an atmosphere of creativity and inclusion that had not been seen for some time. It allowed many people to thrive in ways they would not have been able to before. Great progress was made in civil rights, the cleaning up environment, improving technology, and many other areas of human endeavor.

But there was a cost incurred in this liberation. The "Do Your Own Thing" mentality combined with all the rights movements somehow evolved into the "I'll Get Mine" mindset. Perhaps its genesis is summed up in a statement by Jim Morrison of the rock group The Doors. He said, "Listen, man, I don't know what's gonna happen, but I'm gonna get my kicks before the whole s**thouse goes up in flames."

I'm gonna get my kicks. I'm gonna get mine. A certain theme of self-centeredness pervades these words!

That an entire generation should be indicted because of the rhetoric of its time is unfair, nor is that the intention here. I am smack dab in the middle of the '60s generation myself! Yet, there is no mistaking this subtle thread that was woven into our society's fabric.

Effect

This self-centeredness shows up in a variety of places:

* The intolerance of what could be called "one-issue" movements where there is absolutely no recognition of anyone else's point of view.

  Tom Lehrer illustrated this irony of uncritical thinking in an afterword to his song, "National Brotherhood Week," a brilliant, biting satire on the notion that brotherhood could be celebrated for a week. He quipped, "I am aware of people who are intolerant, *and I can't stand people like that!*"

More seriously, the assassination of doctors who perform abortions by those who proclaim the sacredness of life is tragically ironic.

- The corporate officers who claim to be concerned about their employees, yet conduct massive layoffs at the drop of a hat, while enriching themselves and abusing the privilege and responsibility of their position.

The egos involved here can only be described as *massive*.

- The law-and-order crowd that demands strict enforcement *except when it involves one of their own infractions*.

- A favorite of mine I have dubbed "Kid Sports and the Parents They Have Spawned."

More often than one would like to acknowledge, kid sports is about anything but kids. It is about parents who push their children, manipulate the system, and behave truly outrageously at team meetings, coaches' conferences, and games.

Otherwise normal, pleasant people can become virtually *rabid* when caught up in the vicarious world of kid sports. There are some parents who go so far as to have game plans for their *seven-year-olds* to make the varsity team in high school! Can the Olympics be far behind? Allegedly adult people scream, threaten, interfere, berate, seek vengeance—and then they get mad! All forms of nefarious activities are possible.

How Will It End?

Has the world turned evil? Can Armageddon be upon us?

The answer is an emphatic NO!

Most people are decent.

Most people want what's best for their children (even in kid sports!).

Most people want to excel at something.

Most people want to make a difference—a *positive* difference—in the world.

Most people would love to be a part of something bigger than themselves.

I really don't think we do some of the rotten things we do *intentionally.* No, not at all. Most of us have good intentions, but if we *stopped and considered* the results of some our actions, we might be surprised and dismayed at what we'd discover. It's just that we seldom take the time to do so.

For some reason it is very *macho* to be a man or woman of *action!* It is considered weak and/or foolish to be kind, thoughtful, or merciful.

Perhaps, as I have suggested, this attitude is a remnant of the '60s. Maybe it is an offshoot of being "businesslike." Maybe it's a communist plot, alien intervention, or sunspots! Where or when it originated is beyond the purview of this book.

What I do intend to explore in the pages that follow is the fundamental importance of individuals treating one another humanely. I suggest that the things we call humanity and humane treatment are the first task we should complete, that if we work on and value the human things in life, long-term rewards will follow. *By rewards, I am speaking not only of psychological or spiritual fulfillment, but also of material profits.*

How 'bout that for an example of genuine irony!

Humanity as a Strategic Edge

The young broker was on a "hot" call.

The prospect had just sold his company to a large corporation and had received an enormous amount of stock in the acquiring company. He wanted to diversify his holdings in a rational manner.

He had no end of financial types who were ready to help him.

During the first meeting, the young broker didn't hype any magic strategy and didn't promise the moon or the stars. He just listened to what the prospect was saying about his family, his aspirations, and whatever else was on his mind. The prospect was a talker, and not an eloquent one at that. He was a relatively simple man from a small town. He had worked hard, gotten lucky, and knew it.

At last the new owner of wealth wound himself down, and the broker thought the meeting was coming to an end. Then the prospect said, "You know, one of my oldest managers got some stock, too. He could use some help."

The young broker sighed inwardly, smiled, and said he'd be happy to take the time to meet with the manager.

If the owner was a simple man, the manager was a simpleton. He had done one thing very well for most of his adult life, and that was it. He hadn't been out of the town. He hadn't been well-schooled. What he had been was intensely loyal to his employer. It took a good three hours of probing and listening for the broker to be able to know the manager from the inside out and to ascertain what he could do to be of service. It took another hour to explain the situation so the manager could truly understand what was going on.

During the next several weeks, the young broker took call after call from the manager to answer questions he had answered several times already. It just took a while for the facts to penetrate the manager's mind.

The broker despaired of ever getting business out of either of the men, but he knew he was serving them well by listening to their needs and giving them straight answers.

As it turned out, the manager called one day to inform the young broker that while he appreciated all that he had learned over the preceding weeks, he was going to do business with a friend of his in the small town where the company was located. Said the manager, "I couldn't have done it without you, but I'm just a small-town guy, and I'm more comfortable with someone here than someone in the big city. Hope you understand. And thanks, you were great!"

Well thanks a bunch, thought the young broker. I take the time to listen to you, educate you, and I don't take advantage of you, and "Thank you" is my reward? The dark shadow of murder and mayhem briefly drifted through his mind accompanied by a raging headache, but they didn't remain there long. He wrote off the effort and was determined to plow ahead.

Sometime later and seemingly out of nowhere, the owner called. His statement was short and to the point. He said, "I'm giving you my business. 'As ye treat the least of you, so do ye treat me' You helped my oldest manager as nobody else did. I know I'm in good hands."

Who knew being kind, thoughtful, and merciful could also be profitable?

Of course, there's a catch. Isn't there always a catch?

Embracing humanity does not necessarily mean success today or even tomorrow. It can happen, of course, but it's unlikely. Embracing humanity does mean that with patience and integrity, success is much more likely—and, more likely to be sustained.

Action

Step up and embrace our humanity.

Stepping up and embracing our humanity is such a powerful action to take!

- *Recognize and declare* the part of us that differentiates us from the animal kingdom.

- *Actively search for the best in people and for those things that make them unique.*

- Develop the *unique talents* we discover in *ourselves*.

- Encourage each other to *be* our unique selves.

- Have the courage and *take the time*, both individually and organizationally to be humane.

- Search for and *declare* the higher purpose of our endeavors.

THE PROFESSIONAL
HUMAN BEING—PhB

A worthy goal for all of us is to become a Professional Human Being or PhB.

Think of it! Picture what we could accomplish. Imagine the fulfillment we could feel. Dream of a world where we support each other even as we compete with one another.

It can happen.

What's a Professional Human Being—PhB?

Well, friend, it's a term I made up. And you know what? People resonate with it, especially once they understand what it means.

When I say I made it up, I didn't just grasp at some straw in the wind. I made it up after a half-century of living. I made it up after experiencing heady success and abject failure. After working in every size of organization you can imagine, including my own one-man shop. After raising kids, becoming a grandfather, starting a children's museum, and changing careers at a time when many people are contemplating retirement.

Why did I make it up?

Because from the edge of bankruptcy I've learned what is important—*really* important. And from working inside organizations, I've seen well-meaning leaders do the *stupidest* things! And I have met any number of nice people who feel unfulfilled, frustrated, useless, and, in the age of supposed empowerment, wildly *un*empowered.

And, of course, we've all seen the results of placing numbers ahead of people, power ahead of service, and business ahead of everything else.

The Odd Couple

What an odd combination of words!—Professional Human Being.

The words "professional" and "human being" would seem almost to contradict one another. For example, we hear it said that "She didn't let her emotions get in the way of that tough decision. She was a real professional." On the other hand, when someone makes a distinctly *non*professional move, they're often praised as "a real human being."

The schism between being "professional" and being a "human being" has become so profound, I believe, as to be dangerous— dangerous to our judgment, dangerous to our mental health, and yes, even dangerous to our society.

For example:

- Today we have more means to communicate with one another than ever before, and yet, there are any number of books and studies showing that satisfactory communication is still very difficult to achieve.

- We have more of just about everything than we've ever had in the past, yet we often feel a bit empty and bankrupt.

- We have burglar alarms, consumer laws, and lots of protection, yet we feel vulnerable.

- There are more people in the world than ever before, yet we feel alone and isolated, as if we don't count.

- "The System" seems to be more important than we are, and yet we're hell-bent to improve it and make it even more efficient!

I submit that the human beings we are at home—the ones who can be loving, caring, expressive, humorous, and sometimes just a whole lot of fun—often disappear the minute we walk into our place of business. We mostly forget human quality and perspective and become "professional"—coldly calculating margins, profits, strategies, cost containment, and a healthy dose of CYA,** with little or no regard for the "soft issues" of humanity. The very term "soft issues" implies that those are best handled by people who are *not* professionals. Professionals handle the *hard* issues, and HR (Human Relations) or someone else can handle the *soft* ones! [Note: I mean no disrespect to the fine folks who have chosen careers in HR. You are some of the best PhBs around!]

I question whether human resources are like minerals that one can dig out of bedrock, polish up, and manufacture into increasingly efficient machinery.

Unlike minerals, human resources are human! They're emotional, needy, demanding, and anything but efficient. They can be a detriment to short-term efficiency measurements.

And yet... Human resources are the most important and valuable resources any organization can claim. Calculate the cost of employee turnover (three to five times the employee's total compensation per position, to say nothing of damage to morale) or the cost of lost intellectual capital when an employee leaves, and you'll have a startling dollars-and-cents exercise in the value of that resource.

** Those of you in the corporate world are probably familiar with this term. For those who are not, it means making sure your rear is protected at all times!

On the other hand, with appreciation, encouragement, and proper regard in a positive work environment, these same messy human beings can become dynamic, creative forces for the good of their organization and themselves, producing new ideas, new systems, new structures, and new *profits* that would otherwise never have been conceived or realized!

Is Humanity at Work Truly Effective?

The easy answer is, yes.

I have seen it with my own eyes over a 30-year business career.

My first boss in the investment business practiced humanity at work, and it paid off handsomely for him, the organization, and the recipients.

One of the brokers who started with me was a hard worker, enthusiastic, and totally without connections. He had moved to the city from another state and knew no one. Every day he would get on the phone and call hundreds of people—day after day.

Anyone involved with the brokerage business knows that you spend your day hearing "No" 98 percent of the time. It is not a business that pats you on the back very often. But Steve was nothing if not persistent.

Most rookie brokers have some connections they can tap to show progress, but Steve had none. But he had endless energy and big goals. Still, after months of calling, he had very little to show for his effort.

Earl, the manager, should have let him go. But Earl sensed something in Steve that convinced him to take the gamble and keep paying him, even though Steve wasn't producing enough to cover his overhead.

Earl stood by Steve for almost three years. And it paid off. Big!

Steve became one of the biggest producers in the entire organization and has remained at or near the top ever since, all because his manager thought like a human being instead of a computer.

In all likelihood, that story could not be told today. Most brokerage houses have strict production quotas for new brokers. If those quotas are not met on a prescribed timeline, the broker is let go. The "numbers people" do not understand that *each broker develops at his or her own rate, not according to an arbitrary schedule.* If Steve had started today, he would have been out of the business in six months instead of being one of the biggest producers in the country.

Is Steve an isolated example? No.

In his book, *Good to Great,* Jim Collins conducted a five-year, intensive research study to identify those factors that make companies great. It was no accident that the first factor was what Jim labeled Level Five Leadership. One of the common characteristics of Level Five Leaders is their humility.

Their humility allows them to be PhBs.

PhBs, Level Five Leaders, have a higher purpose than self-promotion. They actively seek people for their unique talents. Humility allows them to serve the people they recruit. Robert Greenleaf wrote extensively about the concept of Servant Leadership. Level Five Leaders are natural PhBs in that they truly want to do everything possible to help their teams succeed, not by interfering and putting their own stamp on events, but by encouraging, listening, and suggesting.

Does humanity at work work? Can a PhB be productive?

Consider this: "if you invested $1 in a mutual fund of the good-to-great companies in 1965, held each company at the general market rate until the date of transition, and simultaneously invested $1 in a general market stock fund, your $1 in the good-to-great fund taken out on January 1, 2000, would have multiplied 471 times, compared to a 56-fold increase in the market."[1]

Just so there is no misunderstanding, Collins lists several other characteristics of good-to-great companies, but it all begins with Level Five Leaders, and Level Five Leaders are PhBs.

1. Jim Collins, *Good to Great,* (New York, HarperCollins Publishers, 2001).

BECOMING
A PhB

To become a Professional Human Being means to achieve improved integration between the people we are at home and the professionals we are at work—to bridge the chasm, to become more aligned and less schizophrenic.

This can be done, I believe, by stepping back from "The System" and looking inward. If we can develop a clear idea of what it is to be a *person*, whatever workplace efficiency is lost in the process will be more than made up for in creativity unleashed and improved relationships established.

Searching for Humanity at Work

She had been working at the bank for almost 20 years. Every day she assembled order requests for paper clips, pens, print cartridges, and all the other paraphernalia a busy office requires. She delivered them smartly and efficiently to the officers and assistants along with a smile and sometimes shared laughter.

But the bank wasn't meeting its numbers, so cuts had to be made. She was an easy one to snip out, so she got her pink slip and disappeared—here on Friday, gone on Monday. We didn't know her total compensation (pay plus benefits), but the billion-dollar revenue bank probably saved a whopping $30,000 by letting her *go. I'm relatively sure that the chairman did not know her name. It was Delores.*

A short time later, I read about the chairman's acquisition of two new pieces of art for the corporate jet—approximately $15,000 a piece. Meanwhile, the officers and assistants wasted precious time wandering about the supply rooms in search of paper clips, pens, print cartridges, and all the other paraphernalia a busy office requires.

Are there organizations that actively promote humanity at work?

If you ask them, virtually all enterprises will say, of course we promote humanity here! Do you think we're all heartless?

However, if you observe the atmosphere of a place and talk to the people who work there, you find more often than not that leadership's perceptions don't match those of their employees at work.

There are two reasons for this divergent view.

First, some organizations really *don't* care about their employees. Employees are a necessary evil to be tolerated to get the job done. The organizations may go through the motions because the latest management gurus have said it's a good thing to do, but it is not at all sincere.

In that way these organizations are like Alfred Hitchcock, the great movie director of thrillers such as *Psycho, Vertigo, The Birds,* and *Rear Window*. Hitchcock loved everything about making movies except having to use actors. Scouting locations, preparing storyboards, planning shoots—all of these were just fine with Hitchcock. But eventually he would have to film actors for the scenes of his movies, and that he found tiresome. Actors were unpredictable and prone to error, and he couldn't control them. If he could have made movies without actors, he would have done so.

Second, and this is true of most organizations, they are so wrapped up in the business and the numbers that regarding employees as people is something to be done if and when time allows, or when there's crisis. It's not that top executives don't think highly of their people. It's just that the needs of the enterprise itself are always a higher priority than the needs of the employees who keep the enterprise afloat. The executives actually do value their employees, but they don't take the time to do much about it. When they do take the time to do something, it is usually quick, formulaic and/or mechanical in nature.

There is hope in these situations.

What's remarkable to me is that certainly in the second case and sometimes even in the first, the people involved are *not* ogres or monsters, but pretty decent folk. Without hesitation, they might do things individually that they would consider *un*businesslike in an organization.

Is someone any less of a human being at work than elsewhere in life? Does he or she deserve to be treated less humanely because of receiving a wage? Does anyone have shallower feelings at work than elsewhere?

There *are* organizations that defy the conventional wisdom and conduct their business and employee relations with a deep sense of purpose and humanity. Sadly, they are the exception, not the rule. It's interesting to note, however, that *these exceptions to the rule tend to be exceptional organizations!*

A Structured Commitment to People

Carolyn Gable founded New Age Transportation. She is a delightful, engaging person.

Carolyn was working as a waitress at the Hyatt Regency at Chicago's O'Hare International Airport in 1982. She was a single mother supporting two children. She had been laid off all summer during renovation of the restaurant, and on the Friday she returned to work, a violent thunderstorm that blew the roof off the building. She learned she would be laid off for an additional six weeks.

With that Carolyn went out and got a job as a customer service representative for a trucking company. After answering customer questions for some time, she wanted something more. She had no training, no experience, and no college education. But she did have a burning desire.

She got a sales job and excelled at it.

Eventually Carolyn went out on her own as a commissioned rep. She worked out of her house and was doing very well until the day her largest customer pulled the account, and she lost 40 percent of her business.

After a week's worth of weeping and gnashing of teeth, Carolyn started her own transportation brokerage company. Now she and her associates handle all the logistics of transportation, distribution, and storage of a variety of merchandise.

That was in 1992. Ten years later Carolyn Gable was named Ernst & Young's Entrepreneur of the Year for 2002. Her company has 47 employees and brought in about $15 million in revenue in 2003.

Carolyn is a feeling person with a deep faith. She also has much experience in living.

"I know what it's like when your child is sick and there's no one else there," she says. She speaks of "...one guiding principle that steers our course: Total and unfailing commitment to the folks who pay the bills around here. And for these loyal clients, we are forever grateful."

Her company works out of an 86,000-square-foot warehouse. The work areas are airy, bright, and filled with inspirational sayings on the walls. The I Care program requires each employee to write at least two thank you notes per week. The entire organization has the adopted the attitude of "Above and Beyond."

Yes, there is the obligatory Employee of the Month program, but at New Age Transportation it is the employees who vote.

Each employee can vote for anyone he or she chooses, but the ballot also requires them to provide three to five reasons for the selection.

Everyone is encouraged to ask themselves, "What have I done spiritually, emotionally, or physically for the community and for fun?"

Carolyn Gage has no apologies for the way her organization runs. She actively seeks the kind of people who are committed to humanity. [See *Good to Great* by Jim Collins: Chapter 3, *First Who... Then What*]. She does not hire someone just to fill a job slot. She hires people who look outside themselves, who want to be part of a community that seeks a higher purpose.

At New Age Transportation, humanity is a stated part of the culture. It is a way of life within the organization. It is part of the vision. It is an integral part of the mission. It permeates *everything* associated with New Age Transportation.

The success of New Age Transportation is not based on education (remember Carolyn never went to college). Although it focuses on profit margins, it is not based *solely* on "the numbers." It is successful because it has created an atmosphere of respect, trust, encouragement, and love. It set out to be this way right from the beginning and has never veered off its course.

An organization can choose to be as humane is it wants to be, and it can formally introduce policies and performances directly into its daily life to achieve that end.

Spontaneous Humanity at Work

I like this next story because it shows what can happen when people really care *and are allowed to act on their caring impulses.*

You would think being kind to someone would be the last thing to trigger potential legal problems, but you would be wrong.

The organization in this story has been recognized as one of the best companies to work for in the country for five years in a row. However, they were hesitant to let me use the corporate name because they worried that what they did for one employee might be taken as something that should be done for *all* employees as a matter of policy. They actually relented and said I could use the company's name, but I have chosen not to because I don't want to cause problems for them, even inadvertently.

Someday I hope that we get over the notion that we have a right to have what someone else has just because they got it, we didn't, and we happen to work at the same place.

Ted's Story

Ted's life changed dramatically and tragically in one day.

In his own words, "In 1995 my then 29-year-old wife was diagnosed with colon cancer. For the next year she fought and inspired people around her, before my treasure became God's. If not for the caring and concern of the people and company I worked for, I would not have made it through that time."

The acts of kindness started within Ted's own team. He has a ready smile and an openness that is infectious. When his team found out what was happening, they rallied around him, helping him when he had to take Katrina for radiation and chemotherapy, bringing food to his house, driving and babysitting as necessary.

At first the company had the good sense to stay out of the way.

Six months into the ordeal, however, Ted went to his boss and asked him what he should do. The organization set him up with an office at home. Another person coordinated the various things Ted needed to do his job and to take care of Katrina.

After seven months the insurance company refused to pay any more bills. Both the company and the university where Katrina worked went to bat for the couple. When the insurance company's customer service department refused to take Ted's calls, the company helped with the bills, and the university threatened to pull its business.

However, Ted's relationship with his team was not all sunshine and roses. At one point they had to sit him down to find out if he was angry with them or if it was just the situation with Katrina that was making him irritable. The fact that they had an honest, open relationship allowed them to communicate with one another.

The company set up a 50 percent matching program to raise money for a scholarship fund in Katrina's name.

When Katrina died, there were far more people than anticipated at the reception at Ted's house after her funeral. Within minutes a truck appeared with a load of extra chairs to set up out in the yard, paid for by the company.

Ted is a very engaging, friendly fellow, which is no doubt one of the reasons that his team and the company responded so willingly to him in his time of deep need. An employee who had worked for him said, "You were the best roof I ever had," meaning Ted had shielded her well from those things that could be distracting to her in accomplishing her job with creativity.

Nevertheless, the organization itself also promotes a culture that allows and encourages this sort of human spontaneity to occur.

By the way, Ted has remarried and moved on with his life and career. He is a happy man.

An organization can allow humanity to be practiced within its borders even if what is done is not part of its written policies.

The Common Element of Humanity at Work

One can cite other examples of how humanity at work can have a galvanizing effect on an organization. But it is important to recognize the common element that runs through virtually all the stories one discovers.

Those organizations that successfully incorporate humanity into the fabric of their existence, whether by defined structure or by simple attitude, do so successfully *because it is an absolutely genuine commitment that comes from the heart, AND it permeates everything they do.*

Unsuccessful Humanity at Work

I have been witness to several employee programs that failed.

The Bad Attitude

One example was a teamwork/sensitivity training at a large bank. The program was quite good, well conducted, and gave us the opportunity to work with a good cross-section of people in the organization. When we returned to work, most of us were eager to put the concepts we had learned into practice. This came to a screeching halt when one of the senior managers declared that vacation was over, and "it's time to get back to work." That attitude killed the enthusiasm of the troops, and a wonderful opportunity for a leap of productivity was lost. Not only was it lost, it actually cast a pall on the entire division. Instead of leaping forward, we all staggered backward.

Just Plain Stupid!

Sometimes just plain stupidity will kill a perfectly good plan.

I was working for a large financial services firm when they decided (to their credit) to set up a profit-sharing program for those employees who were not partners. I *know* they were sincere about it because I was involved in the many hours of meetings we conducted in an attempt to make the program fair for all involved. When the program was announced, there was real excitement in the air.

Three weeks later at a meeting in Chicago, the leadership announced the revenue goals for the next year. I don't know if there had been heavy drinking the night before or if someone had spiked the coffee with amphetamines, but the goal was colossal—a 40 percent increase! "We're going to make a pre emptive strike on the competition," exclaimed the fearless and clueless leaders. Despite struggling with freshman calculus in college, I do know something about numbers. Let's see—when most of the work is charged by the hour, one wonders how they ever thought we could achieve a 40 percent increase in revenue, especially when there was no mention of new hires. This was a true s-t -r-e--t--c--h goal!

It was also a ridiculously impossible goal.

When we announced the revenue goal to the troops, the *universal* reaction was, "You really weren't serious about the profit-sharing were you?" Nothing we could say or do would convince anyone to the contrary. A great opportunity and an enormous amount of effort were wasted and goodwill dissipated simply because of an act of thoughtless derring-do.

Humanity at Work is TOTAL Commitment

Actively promoting humanity at work is an all-encompassing effort. Every action, every strategy, every policy, indeed every word is important. You can talk to machinery all you want— curse it, caress it, kick it—do anything you want to it, and it will remain silent, stoic, and uncomplaining.

Not so with all of us messy little human creatures.

We require constant care and feeding, complimenting, back-patting, hand-holding, and other forms of acknowledgment of our existence. God, but we surely are an inefficient tool of commerce!

But we have our strengths.

I'll tell you what—the next time you need some input, go to your copier and see what you get. The next time you want to share a triumph, turn on your computer and wait for its enthusiasm to boot up. And the next time you want to find a truly inspired idea, perhaps your electronic calendar will light up with one.

Or maybe not.

Not only are human beings the only creative resource you have in your organization, they also supply much of the stuff that both you and the organization need to keep growing, expanding, and providing fulfillment for the marketplace *and for yourselves.*

The power of the human mind and the human soul is astounding. Like precious stones, however, you just don't find them lying around easy to pick up. They require work—constant work. To constantly get the most out of people is to appreciate them for who they are, as they are. That's what takes concentrated effort by each of us. It is a positive attitude toward people that each one of us can *choose* to take. If we make that positive choice, then there is very little we cannot accomplish together. Those values of loyalty, hard work, creativity, productivity—attributes that most organizations want to see from their employees—are all possible with the basic commitment to humanity for those you work with.

Do you want loyalty? *Demonstrate loyalty!*

Do you want hard work? *Work hard!*

Do you want creativity? *Be creative! And allow others to be creative, too!*

Do want a sense of community? *Act with a sense of community!*

Goethe said it best: "We are shaped and fashioned by what we love."

We cannot ignore the numbers—no profits = no work at all. To be sure, EBITDA, gross margins, market share, customer service, market research, and all other terms and tools of business are important. But business terms and tools alone will not sustain an organization.

Only people can do that.

Reading for extra credit *(for complete publisher information see Consolidated Reading List on page 123)*

☞ *Good to Great,* Jim Collins

☞ *The Serving Leader,* Ken Jennings and John Stahl-Wert

To Be a Professional Human Being

Level Five leaders are almost always professional human beings. They are looking at something bigger than themselves. They *build* a legacy without *worrying* about the legacy. They want others to join them in excelling at something with a high purpose.

It takes great effort and skill to be a Professional Human Being (PhB).

Fortunately, the skills can be learned, and the effort is ours for the making.

And unlike becoming a doctor, lawyer, or physicist, becoming a Professional Human Being does not require highly specialized and esoteric schooling. *Anyone can become a PhB.*

Intuitively, we can feel that the dynamics of humanity are powerful. This power is not limited to Level Five leaders or presidents or the rich. It is accessible *right now* to anyone that seeks it.

In fact, being a PhB is as important to followers as it is to leaders. As we learn, we realize that we can hold our happiness and fulfillment at work within our own grasp. The attitudes *we* choose, the way *we* regard our colleagues, the way *we* actually conduct ourselves in whatever task we are assigned—these are all things *we* can control.

Also, to be a PhB means that we can appreciate the strengths and weaknesses of our own leaders. We sometimes forget in this age of hype and aggrandizement that those in positions of leadership are, after all, human themselves. Although they may not show it, they have hopes, fears, vexing problems, great celebrations, triumphs and tragedies in their lives just as we do in ours. They make mistakes—sometimes really big ones—as we all do.

Whether you are a leader or a follower, putting humanity first—being a PhB—is equally important.

Being a PhB is the great equalizer.

Being a PhB is also the great energizer.

Humanity puts everyone on the same level playing field. Humanity allows egos to disappear and higher purpose to emerge in their place. It is a more efficient way of operating because less time is spent on "managing" people, and more time is spent on doing productive work.

So it would seem appealing and make a certain amount of sense to populate our organizations and our lives with PhBs and to actively work in that direction ourselves.

That is the purpose of the balance of this book.

I don't propose to introduce anything of a new and startling nature. As King Solomon said, "There is nothing new under the sun." There is great value, however, in reviewing what we already know with a new perspective.

Most professions require continuing education to maintain the degree. Maintaining a PhB is no exception. The learning process never ceases because like life itself, being a Professional Human Being is a long, continuous journey.

So, for those first timers and for those seeking continuing

education, the rest of this book is devoted to the elements that make up a Professional Human Being (PhB). Call it a fundamental course about what you already know intuitively.

And by the way, I have already given you an *A* in this course. This *A* is a gift that was given to me by Benjamin and Rosamund Stone Zander in their marvelous book, *The Art of Possibility*.

Please note the A I have passed on to you "is not an expectation to live up to, but a possibility to live into."[1]

You have the material in front of you. Understand that you are to share it with *everyone*. Looking over your colleague's shoulder is expected and encouraged. Please know that you will be given plenty of time for the all assignments at the end of this course. Take the rest of your life if you need it.

You may begin...........................Now!

---

1. Rosamund Stone Zander and Benjamin Zander, *The Art of Possibility*, (Boston: Harvard Business School Press, 2000).

COURSE
OUTLINE**

1. **Value Other People**
2. **Integrity**
3. **Choose a Positive Attitude.**
4. **Understand and Practice Humility.**
5. **Be Open**
6. **Let Go**
7. **Laugh!**
8. **Celebrate, celebrate! Dance to the music!**
9. **Help Others.**
10. **Stand by your word.**
11. **Love Yourself**
12. **Find Your Purpose and Live!**

Conclusions

Assignments

** Format Note: Each lesson appears first in compact form (one or two pages—max) with commentary following. If you want to know more and dig a little deeper, read the commentary. For those of you who choose to do so and are marching through life at a more modest pace, congratulations! You're already onto something special.

Also, you may notice that I have used quotes more than once and suggested books for further reading more than once.

This is intentional.

VALUE
Other People

Use what talents you possess;
the woods would be very silent if no birds sang
except those that sang the best.

—Henry Van Dyke

Do the best you can with what you've got where you are.

—George Washington Carver

You are absolutely unique. In the history of the world there has never been another you. And there never will be another you.

But if you are absolutely unique, then *all* people must be absolutely unique. As a PhB, your task is to seek out that uniqueness in every human encounter you have. Through close and active listening, by observation, by *wanting* to know, you are charged with finding that element—however tiny—that makes a person unique. Once this uniqueness has been uncovered, the PHB sets about to highlight and celebrate it.

Every person has a story. Elicit it. Listen to it. Celebrate it.

Efficiency, systems, and machines are nice, but they're not unique. They can be duplicated. They have no essence. They have no heart. They have no story. They cannot comfort the human soul. That is solely the province of inefficient, warm and wonderful human beings.

What can YOU do?

✓ Take the time and the interest to know co-workers as people.

✓ Actively look for unique facets of the people around you.

✓ After listening to their stories and discovering their uniqueness, think about how it can be celebrated, enhanced, and put to good use.

Reading for extra credit

✏ *Loving What Is,* Byron Katie and Stephen Mitchell

✏ *The Diversity Advantage,* Lenora Billings-Harris

Be yourself; no base imitator of another, but your best self. There is something which you can do better than another. Listen to the inward voice and bravely obey that. Do the things at which you are great, not what you were never made for.

—Ralph Waldo Emerson

Commentary

Isn't it ironic that we humans, who have dominion over this planet, who have conquered the wind, water, air, and atmosphere, left the confines of Mother Earth, moved mountains, and diverted mighty rivers—isn't it ironic that we are the most helpless of all mammals when we are born. Not only that, we remain the most helpless of all mammals for a very long time thereafter.

Yet when we grow up, we differ greatly amongst ourselves.

Think about it. All leopards have spots, all elephants have trunks, all dogs have the same characteristics of their breed—in other words, if you have seen one lion, you've seen them all. Scientists and naturists will probably take issue with this train of thought, but let's face it—unless you're paying close attention, most animals of a given species look almost identical to one another.

Not the human being.

No matter the race, religion, or country of origin, human beings are unique unto themselves. We each have the same number of body elements, but oh how different we all look from one another. The colors and shapes of faces and bodies, fingers and toes are endlessly pieced together in astonishingly different ways.

So here's the question: If our physical selves are so unique, shouldn't it stand to reason that our inner beings should be just as unique?

It is the quest of the PhB to find and celebrate that uniqueness.

Some gifts and talents are small. Some people have been blessed with gifts and talents in abundance. The PhB is always curious and eager to discover an individual's gifts and talents and to bring them to the forefront.

This discovery often takes time, and it could be categorized as inefficient, but the rewards can be huge. On a practical basis, when human creativity is unleashed, an organization can come to life and become an exciting place of progress and innovation. In the short run there may some inefficiency due to the trial and error involved in any creation, but the long-term benefits can be astounding. Not only can the organization leap forward, but employee morale may well become stronger and more upbeat as well. People love to arrive at work knowing that there is another challenge for them to face. This can be achieved only if they're allowed to contribute the gifts and talents that are uniquely theirs.

On a personal level, the enjoyment and fulfillment experienced by someone who unlocks the talent of another is simply priceless.

INTEGRITY
Be a Seeker of Truth,
not a Manilpulator
of Facts

Whenever you do a thing,
act as if all the world were watching.

—Thomas Jefferson

S*pin* is the word of this era. The raw truth is thought to be relative to each person's view of it. Under this definition the truth can be spun by manipulating the facts—including some, omitting others—and by exhibiting the emotion chosen to be most useful for the spinner.

The PhB looks for the Truth. The Truth indeed may have many perspectives, but it is still the Truth. What is important is to seek the Truth without worrying about the spin, without trying to gain personal advantage by twisting and torturing the facts. Eventually, almost everyone sees through the manufactured tale of the "spinmeister," and eventually no one has much respect for such a person.

Integrity, on the other hand, stands on its own. Eventually, the person with integrity is seen as solid and trustworthy. Here is an example of efficiency! A person with integrity can be believed, and there is no time wasted in trying to "interpret" what is said.

Study the etymology of the word *integrity.* Meditate on its various meanings. Understand the rock solid foundation that integrity can build.

From Merriam-Webster's Online Dictionary:

>**Main Entry:** in·teg·ri·ty
>**Pronunciation:** in-'te-gr&-tE
>**Function:** *noun*
>**Etymology:** Middle English integrite, from Middle French & Latin; Middle French *integrité,* from Latin *integritat-, integritas,* from *integr-, integer* entire
>**Date:** 14th century

1 : firm adherence to a code of especially moral or artistic values: INCORRUPTIBILITY
2 : an unimpaired condition: SOUNDNESS
3 : the quality or state of being complete or undivided: COMPLETENESS
>**synonym** see HONESTY

Although the first two definitions are excellent, the PhB naturally looks to the third. A state of being complete or undivided is the base on which to build a life that matters. Being in such a state doesn't rule out questioning, searching, and challenging as a way of being, but integrity serves as the baseline of comparison.

Many of the woes suffered by modern corporate America could have been avoided completely had the boards of directors, CEOs, auditors, and regulators simply sought the truth and acknowledged it. Instead, many corporate leaders attempt to be clever and cute with their statements, holding their employees, investors, and customers by the ears while socking it to them in another location. What a pity!

Maintaining one's integrity can be a trial even in a society that values it. In the present age, the PhB knows that maintaining integrity is very often a lonely, unpopular vigil where one can even be subject to attack and scorn for "being naïve." Nobody said being a PhB was an easy ride.

What can YOU do?

✓ Don't speak unless you have something to say.

✓ Be more interested in the truth than the deadline.

✓ Be pleasant and confident.

✓ Constantly check to see that your personal beliefs and your organizational objectives are aligned. When they are not aligned, follow your beliefs.

Reading for extra credit

✒ *What Matters Most—The Power of Living Your Values,* Hyrum W. Smith

*One stumble is enough to deface the character
of an honorable life.*

—L. Estrange

We cannot restore integrity and morality to our society
until each of us—singly and individually—
takes responsibility for our actions.

—Harry Emerson Fosdick

Commentary

The finest example of integrity I have ever encountered occurred within my own family and involved my great-grandfather. His story is one that has shaped and defined me, and has been a wonderful reference point for all of my life. I hope you will indulge me and allow me to relate his story to you.

Francis A. Bean was a miller in south central Minnesota. He was known as an honest, hardworking man.

At the age of 50, he went bankrupt. The combination of monopoly railroad shipping rates and an economic panic that swept through the county did him in. Since the life expectancy was about 47 years in those days, this was a devastating blow.

Bean picked himself up and began again. He borrowed money from his brother-in-law and got back into the business of milling. He approached the First National Bank of Minneapolis for a loan. The president of the bank said to him, "Frank, there is no way I should be making the loan—absolutely no way whatsoever. But I know you, and I know you are honest and a hard worker, so I'm going to approve your loan request." [Intercommentary comment: There is no way—*absolutely no way whatsoever*—that loan could be made today.]

With that loan, Bean proceeded to build a mill. He didn't stop building for 20 years. By then he'd built a very fine company. He was wealthy and well-respected in the community.

At the age of 71, two weeks before Christmas in December 1911, he informed his family that he had to take a business trip. He said he might not make it home for Christmas, but he was sure it was going to be a great Christmas—one of the best ever. With that he left, never telling them or anyone else where he was going or what he was planning to do.

His first stop was at the offices of Bemis Bag Company. He walked into the office and went directly to accounts receivable.

"I've come to pay a debt," he said. "It's an old one."

The clerk looked in the books and informed Bean that he had no debts outstanding.

"Yes, I do," said Bean. "Look further back, say 20 years ago."

Sure enough, there was an entry that indicated Polar Star Milling owed Bemis Bag Company a fair amount of money, but there was also a notation that the amount had been written off because of Bean's bankruptcy.

"You don't owe us anything. That debt was written off *years* ago," said the Accounts Receivable clerk.

"No, I'm going to pay my debt," declared Bean.

And pay his debt he did—the amount he originally owed, *plus 6 percent interest for 20 years.*

Francis Bean repeated this scene with every company he owed from his bankruptcy 20 years before. He paid back every one their original accounts receivable, plus 6 percent interest for 20 years.

This story should have been lost forever, because Francis Bean did not want anyone to know what he was doing. This exercise was for his private satisfaction and not for publicity. The only reason we know of it at all is because one of those companies he paid called the Minneapolis newspaper.

These were debts that by law he did not have to pay. These were debts that had been written off many years before. But these were debts that he felt he owed, that he said he would pay, and therefore he would pay *because he gave his word that he would.*

The PhB lives up to his word, plain and simple. Instead of trying to spin his way out of a situation gone wrong, he or she owns up to it no matter how painful or avoidable.

One can imagine how much money, heartache, embarrassment, and incarceration could be avoided if people would simply own up to what's theirs.

CHOOSE A
Positive Attitude ▼

Life is not the way it's supposed to be.
It's the way it is. The way you cope with it
is what makes the difference.

—Virginia Satir, social worker

The cherries and the pits exist together. You pick a cherry; you get a pit with it. No one likes the pits. They're hard, tasteless, and can crack your teeth. You spit them out, or say that something is "the pits".

But we need the pits. That's why they come with every cherry. Think about it. Without the pit, would we enjoy the cherry as much? There is nothing like chewing on a pit to understand and appreciate the soft, sweet flesh of the cherry. Besides, if we didn't have the pits, where would future cherries come from?

We have a choice. We can complain bitterly about the pit that is in every cherry, *or* we can note its presence, take care we don't bite down too hard on it, use it to appreciate the better part of the fruit, and plant it, find a use for it, or discard it.

This choice—to approach life each day with a positive attitude—is one that cannot be stolen from us or denied us. It is our choice alone to make.

It is also our sole responsibility. Said another way, the PhB understands that, like forgiveness, *a positive attitude is an individual choice, not an emotion.*

What can YOU do?

✓ Make the effort to understand what is really going on around you.

✓ Look at things as they are, then choose the positive outlook. This gives you a baseline.

✓ Look for ways to improve yourself, your situation, and the situation of those around you.

Reading for extra credit

✏ *Man's Search for Meaning,* Viktor E. Frankl

✏ *Nuts! Southwest Airlines Crazy Recipe for Business and Personal Success,* Kevin & Jackie Freiberg

✏ *Fish!* Stephen C. Lundin, Harry Paul, and John Christensen

✏ *Loving What Is,* Byron Katie

✏ *Principled Profit,* Shel Horowitz

> *Let us not bankrupt our todays by paying interest*
> *on the regrets of yesterday and by borrowing*
> *in advance the troubles of tomorrow.*
>
> **—Ralph W. Sockman—minister**

Commentary

"Put on a Happy Face" is happy song from the Broadway and Hollywood hit *Bye, Bye, Birdie*, a spoof of Elvis Presley's induction into the U. S. Army. "Gray skies are gonna clear up," goes the song, "Put on a happy face!"

That's not what we're talking about here, although parenthetically speaking, it's not the worst habit one could develop.

No, the concept here is one that Viktor Frankl discovered in the Nazi concentration camps during World War II.

Frankl was an Austrian psychiatrist. A Jew, he was sent to the camps where he spent the entire war. He met his wife in the camps but also lost his entire family.

As horrendous as the concentration camps were, for a psychiatrist no other laboratory could provide as harsh a look at the human condition, and Frankl, partly for his own survival, was fascinated by the behavior he observed.

What struck him most vividly was the fact that some people who should have died lived, and others who should have lived died. The latter were often younger men in comparatively good physical condition. After a short time in the camp, they would go to bed one night and be dead in the morning. It was as if they just let go of their lives. Yet there were others, older and more infirm, who got up day after day and went on.

How could this be? Frankl wondered. What makes a man literally give up and die, while another man survives, albeit grimly?

What he concluded was that those who had a purpose also had a reason to live. Sometimes the purpose was noble—to find my family, to live to tell the world what happened here. Sometimes the purpose was not so noble—I will stay alive for the opportunity to kill that brute guard with my bare hands and wipe that sadistic grin off his ugly face.

Noble or ignoble, a sense of purpose gave a prisoner a reason to live. And with a sense of purpose came an attitude, or better said, a choice of attitude. These men found themselves in a situation over which they had absolutely no control, but the one thing they *could* choose and control was their attitude. This was Frankl's great discovery:

> A person can lose just about every freedom and every thing—movement, money, possessions, family, clothes, even parts of the body. *But the one freedom that cannot be taken away is the freedom to choose the attitude one brings to the situation he or she is in.*

If inmates of the most horrific concentration camps in human history can stay alive by exercising their freedom of attitude, then we should be able to accomplish at least as much in our own relatively comfortable lives.

The PhB is one who is fond of Virginia Satir's quote that begins this lesson. It is repeated here, for it virtually defines the human condition.

Life is not the way it's supposed to be. It's the way it is. The way you cope with it is what makes the difference.

UNDERSTAND
And Practice
Humility

*None are so empty as those
who are full of themselves.*

—Andrew Jackson

The PhB embraces humility. Humility is a derivative of the word *humble*. It is also frequently misunderstood or derided.

Humility is not toadyism. It is not self-effacement. It is "free from ostentation, elegance, or affectation." In other words being humble does not forfeit the PhB's right to be assertive or to hold deep beliefs. It is more an attitude toward others and life in general.

If everyone is truly unique and has some gifts to be recognized and shared, then the PhB is obligated to honor each person. It is difficult to honor anyone genuinely if one is haughty, proud, and uncaring. And these things throw the world out of balance.

Many a man or woman has been so wrapped up in their own personalized glory that they have failed to see the glory in their fellow life-travelers.

Humility, then, is that state of mind that switches the focus from the self to the world outside of the self, and it particularly focuses on the needs of others as people, not mere employees, customers, ethnic classes, etc.

The PhB practices noticing the world outside the self and tuning in to the sensitivities of those he finds there. He is open to viewpoints new and different from his own, and he actively seeks to understand them, even if the experience is unnerving and unsettling. A new adventure abounds with every new person he meets.

And the PhB enjoys the journey of discovery.

What can YOU do?

✓ Keep your mouth closed and your ears open when having a conversation with others.

✓ Listen, encourage, praise.

✓ Don't talk too much about yourself.

✓ Look for a person's strength and encourage it.

✓ Note a person's weakness and work positively to correct it.

✓ When reprimanding, do so positively so as to perform a correction, NOT a vindication.

✓ Be courteous.

Reading for extra credit

✎ *Level 5 Leadership: The Triumph of Humility and Fierce Resolve (HBR OnPoint Enhanced Edition)*, Jim Collins

✎ *The Diversity Advantage*, Lenora Billings-Harris

Nothing is ever lost by courtesy. It is the cheapest of pleasures, costs nothing, and conveys much.

—Erastus Wiman

Commentary

I am a great fan of the comedian Jonathan Winters. His off-beat and sometimes maniacal wit, like much humor, is based on human fragility.

During the 1964 presidential campaign, he put out a record called *Whistle Stopping with Jonathan Winters*, in which he played an array of diverse characters—a veritable cross-section of the voting public. One of his signature characters, Maude Frickert, represented the senior citizens, and Lance Loveguard represented the ultra-liberal. Sally Sweetwater was the typical American housewife (this was 1964, mind you!). He played her as a soft-spoken, gentle woman with a son named Howie. She invited the interviewer to "have a seat on the sofa next to the knotty pine pillow from Niagara Falls."

When asked what she wanted to see in a presidential candidate, Sally said, "I see a God-fearing man—not afraid of God, but he knows if he screws up, God'll get him."

That's a little how I look at the person with true humility.

They know many things. They know many people. They have great power. They contribute time and money to their community. They could blow you away with all their accomplishments—but they don't.

Instead, when they're with you, they are truly interested in you. Unless you press them, they simply don't talk about themselves. They know that whatever they have accomplished is always in the past, and what really counts is now, in this very moment.

Sandy Bemis was such a person. Sandy had a wonderfully dry sense of humor that was at times so subtle you could miss it. His accomplishments were monumental. Frankly, I could never keep track of all the things he'd done, but I know that he did so much work for the Minnesota Orchestra that it performed at his funeral service.

And the Minnesota Orchestra was just one of many, many projects he worked on.

To me, he was a friend. He listened intently and humbly offered his advice if I asked for it. He was honest and straightforward and as unaffected a person as I have ever known.

I don't think I ever heard the man complain about anything. The closest he came to voicing a complaint to me was just once in the last months of his life. I saw him on the street and asked how things were going.

"Pretty good," he said, "But I have to run. I'm late for an appointment."

"Must be awfully important," I quipped, "If you can't take minute for *moi*."

He chuckled and said, "Dialysis. I've been going a couple of times a week."

"Oh, Sandy, I'm sorry, I didn't know."

"That's OK," he said. "It keeps me off the street, although I think I'd rather be on the street!"

With that he strode off for his dialysis treatment.

I'm sure his physical condition laid heavily on his mind. Otherwise, he would never have "burdened" me by letting me know where he was going.

Sometimes I think *humility* is a synonym for class.

BE
OPEN

The most beautiful thing we can experience is the mysterious.

—Albert Einstein

Be open to the entire universe and everything in it.

There are powers and forces at work here, and they can be tapped into if the mind is open and quiet.

The PhB knows that the universe is much bigger than any one person. And there are ideas and thoughts much different from what he or she expects or is used to.

Be open to the possibility of new growth and understanding. Be open to the possibility of learning new truths. Be open to the world around you. Be open to nature, people, ideas and thoughts.

To be open is to make a choice. It is an attitude of learning, and it takes a conscious assignment of time. The PhB knows that this is time well spent.

The PhB knows that it is important to find his or her unique place and purpose in the universal scheme. There are values to be discovered and incorporated so that they are truly owned. But along the way, openness to those things that are not theirs alone is also critical. The PhB does not need to incorporate every new idea into his or her belief system. Rather, he or she uses these new thoughts and ideas to test his own and more important, to understand other people.

Being open to possibilities is how the PhB learns.

Those who are closed miss much. Those who are closed do not learn and grow. Fortunately, the PhB knows that the power of the universe can not be turned aside. Like it or not, people learn because of this!

But why struggle to learn all the time when just by being open, one can be exposed to so much that is possible?

Be open.

What can YOU do?

✓ Ask about new ideas suggested by others.

✓ Listen fully to suggestions without commentary.

✓ Take the time to contemplate suggestions and ideas before responding to them.

✓ Read widely.

✓ Find regular quiet time to open yourself to the possibilities that are all around you.

Reading for extra credit

✐ *The Art of Possibility,* Benjamin Zander & Rosamund Stone Zander

✐ *Synchronicity—The Inner Path of Leadership,* Joseph Jaworksi

✐ *Meaning—The Secret of Being Alive,* Cliff Havener

How can we ever hope to grasp the deeper possibilities of life, and lead invigorated or meaningful days, if we're all dashing around nonstop like water bugs on the surface of a swirling river?

—Robert K. Cooper

Commentary

I realize that the concept of being open to the universe can be a difficult one for the well-educated and well-motivated person.

I graduated from Amherst College, an intellectual bastion of the East. I can't prove it, but I think their mission was to scrape away every last vestige of intuition I possessed. They very nearly succeeded, but I'm happy to say, I have made a pretty good recovery. To be fair, Amherst excelled in scraping away old perceptions about how to learn so that you could independently learn to seek, challenge, and learn anew. In truth, my college education, while painful at times, prepared me well to accept the possibilities of being open.

There should be no misunderstanding about intuition versus rational thought. Both are absolutely necessary in this life. However, of the two, intuition (being open) usually gets the short straw. It seems that if one can't *prove* something through the rational thought process, then it must not exist.

Balderdash! (Believe me, I wanted to write something with a bit more punch and spice, but rational thought prevented me from doing so.)

Being open to what the universe has to offer goes hand in glove with the concept of humility. Who are we to say that we know all there is to know? In fact, it is rational to think that we don't.

When Gene Roddenberry created the original *Star Trek* television show, he wanted to know if it was possible that there might be other worlds that possessed Earth-like atmospheres. His point was that producing a show where all the characters were forced to wear space suits would be a creative nightmare.

Roddenberry consulted with a number of scientists who assured him that the mathematical possibility was that in the entire universe, there could be as many as *six billion* Earth-like planets. Roddenberry happily created a franchise that has endured almost 50 years as of this writing.

One of my coaching friends with whom I studied for my coaching certification made a rather startling suggestion to me. She was coaching me (being coached is a major part of learning to coach), and the conversation had turned to how I could go into business for myself. At the time I had been in the investment business for over 25 years.

"All I really want to do is coach and speak. That's it," I said. "Keeping books, drawing up business plans, public relations—none of that has any appeal to me whatsoever. Just let me do what I love to do!"

She is a very competent, highly educated coach with the Boeing Company, so she floored me with her next statement.

"John," she said, "You don't have to do all those things yourself. Just put it out to the universe and see what comes back."

"What do you mean?" I asked, not sure I had heard her correctly.

"What I mean is that all you have to do is let people know what you want to do. Put your intentions out there, *and then have confidence that the answers and solutions will come to you.*" [Emphasis mine]

And you know what? It worked!

Yes, I had a vision and a plan, but I have to say that until I threw it (and myself, for that matter) out into the universe, the vision and plan were still-life objects in a moving picture. By stating my intentions *and being open*, the answers and solutions did indeed begin to present themselves to me.

Here's what happened within three weeks of that conversation:

- I had a company.
- I had a Web site.
- I had a logo.

- I met a publisher.
- I was hired for my first speaking engagement.
- I framed the idea for this book you are reading.

Within six months of that conversation:

- I left the investment business.
- I became a full-time speaker and coach.
- I met some of the most wonderful, sharing people I have ever encountered.

Being open may not be such a goofy concept after all!

LET
Go

Life is a Gift, not a Prize.

—Rick Beneteau

The brighter you are, the more you have to learn.

—Don Herold

The PhB knows how to let go.

In a world that seems to demand that we excel, that we grab hold of our own situation and states in no uncertain terms, we hold all the keys to success in our own two hands, "Let Go" seems like an absurd bit of advice.

But control is illusory. Those forces in the universe that were discussed a mere chapter ago have a way of letting the simple human being know that he or she controls very little.

In fact, the more a person tries to seize and cling to power, the more difficult it becomes to maintain the grasp until all attempts to do so become frantic.

The PhB recognizes the irony here. To retain power is to loosen the grip. Indeed, in the organization, great leaders freely give away power. To *empower* someone is literally *give* them power. Amazingly enough, there is limitless power to be given.

Power is not the only thing to let go of.

There are illusions to be shed, bad habits to break, mistaken ideas to slough off. In short, there are many things that can be let go of, simply by deciding to do so.

The PhB understands that what is let go by one person is not necessarily the same as that which is let go by another. It is *the willingness to let go of everything* that is important here. Not everything that is loosely held will disappear. And you will know what should be maintained in your life because it will stay with you once loosed.

What can YOU do?

- Understands, but be unimpressed with your own power.
- Share your power.
- Loosen your grip on *everything.*

Reading for extra credit

- *Loving What Is,* Byron Katie with Stephen Mitchell

Take yourself less seriously.

—Odette Pollar, Writer

*"Rest is not idleness, and to lie sometimes on the grass
on a summer day listening to the murmur of water,
or watching the clouds float across the sky,
is hardly a waste of time."*

—Sir John Lubbock

Commentary

Most of what one must let go of are thoughts. I could add erroneous beliefs, as well, but beliefs are just thoughts, are they not?

I have often dealt with people who insisted on harboring thoughts of hate or revenge. Someone has wronged them, and now they carry a deep, dark seed of inner rage within themselves wherever they go.

Let's assume that the wrong suffered was legitimate. Now then, by clinging to these dark thoughts of hate and revenge, just who is it that is suffering?

The perpetrator? No, he or she probably hasn't given you a second thought since "the incident".

Who then are these thoughts hurting?

I'll give you hint. If you harbor thoughts such as these, look in the mirror and see the most pathetic victim of your recriminations.

How many times were you wronged by this individual?—probably just once.

Now think about this…How many times have you been wronged *in your own mind by playing the original wrong over and over again?*—probably dozens and dozens of times. So who is inflicting the damage to you?—not the perpetrator. YOU are!

All your evil schemes of revenge, all those great moments of absolute victory over the vile, grotesque monster that "done you wrong", certainly aren't hurting him or her. They are totally unaware of your inner turmoil. In fact, if the "perp" knew how miserable and upset you were, he'd probably be delighted! Not only are you hurting yourself, you are probably making the those around you uncomfortable or irritated because of your constant dwelling on something that is over and done with.

OK, try this. Ask yourself the question, what would I be like if I got rid of these thoughts of revenge?

Chances are you would be at peace with yourself. You would feel better. You could be more creative and productive. You would probably be much more pleasant to be around.

So tell me. Isn't this thought something to let go of?

Take the time to analyze your thoughts, especially those that seem to bother you or cause you mental anguish. Loosen your grip and let them go.

LAUGH

Wrinkles should merely indicate where smiles have been.

Mark Twain, humorist and writer

Laughter is powerful.

Did you know that when you laugh, your blood pressure drops, there is a reduction in the level of stress hormones, and an increase in the level of antibodies in your body? Not only that, laughter releases endorphins into your bloodstream. Endorphins make you feel good. These are the same endorphins that are released when you exercise. In fact, a person who laughs as many times a day as a child has experienced the equivalent of fifteen minutes of aerobic exercise. Who needs a health club?

There is always something to laugh about.

Cable TV has comedians on almost every hour of the day and night. *I Love Lucy, Cheers, M*A*S*H,* and countless other sitcoms are shown endlessly. Tune in and tune yourself up.

The PhB doesn't *need* a TV, however. It's OK to have one, but the PhB can simply observe life and discover endless absurdities all around. How about those horns that sound when a truck is in reverse gear? Good idea, but don't you think it's a bit absurd to then issue ear plugs for the noise?

The humor can also be dark. Death and disability are not light subjects in themselves, but some of the situations that result from them can only be met with laughter. The PhB knows that often times there is a fine line between laughter and insanity, and that laughter can be the lifeline in an ugly storm.

Once again, there is a choice to make. In any given situation one can choose to laugh. Or not.

What can YOU do?

✓ Lighten up!

✓ Read the funnies *every day.*

✓ Be serious about your job and mission, but never fail to see and appreciate the absurdity life offers up.

✓ Smile easily and often.

✓ Enjoy humor on all levels.

✓ Uses humor as a booster, not a weapon.

Read for extra credit

✏ *Never Act Your Age: Play the Happy Childlike Role Well at Every Age,* Dale L. Anderson, Arden Moore

✏ *Becoming a Humor Being—The Power to Choose a Better Way,* Steve Rizzo

✏ *"But I'm Not Funny!"* David Glickman

> *If you find yourself in a hole,*
> *the first thing to do is stop digging.*
>
> **—Will Rogers**

> *Cheerfulness gives elasticity to the spirit.*
>
> **—Samuel Smiles, writer**

Commentary

f I had one piece of advice for working Americans, especially those in positions of leadership, it would be, *lighten up and don't take yourself so damn seriously!*

Oh, I understand how serious business can be, and how tough decisions have to be made. Lord knows I've had to make some of them myself.

But I contend that one needn't maintain that tough, grim visage at all times. In fact, it's quite healthy and at times absolutely necessary to step back, lighten up, and lift the burden, even if just for a moment or two.

—Diatribe—

Who are you kidding, anyway? Are you personally *so* important to all that goes on in the world? I often wonder if those leaders who love to expound on how sharp, tough, cutting edge, productive, and just plain wonderful they are, would be nearly as effective if the people who work for them refused to show up to work one day. Trust me, Wonder Leaders, the world will continue to evolve without you (and in some cases despite you!). But I digress.

—End of Diatribe—

I learned the value of laughter from my drill sergeant during Army basic training. Yes, you read that correctly—my drill sergeant during Army basic training.

For those of you who have never enjoyed the military lifestyle, basic training is, simply put, that course of study that teaches you how to kill the enemy. You learn to shoot your rifle (the preferred way to dispatch the foe), but you also learn about bayonets, hand grenades, pugil sticks, and hand-to-hand combat—in short, everything a soldier needs to know for defense and death.

This is *not* your local comedy club.

In addition, the Army has a way of quickly breaking you of your individuality and forming a sense of unity among the corps. It's really quite amazing how quickly a soldier bonds with his new buddies when they're all subject to the same torturous routines every day.

When I arrived at basic training, my drill sergeant was waiting for me—waiting for me *personally!* For one solid week he seemed to be my personal drill sergeant. Every dirty job was assigned to me. If there was all-night duty, I got it. After a week, he took me aside (I thought perhaps he was finally going to kill me) and asked me to help him with the rest of the platoon. Thus a strange relationship was formed—the white, college-educated recruit from the North and the black, eighth-grade dropout, Army lifer from the South, working together as a close-knit team.

What I discovered by working so closely with my beloved drill sergeant is that he was one of the best leaders I have ever met. In this tough environment, charged with the grim job of teaching death and destruction, Drill Sergeant Morning got the most out of us by lightening up when he needed to.

No, he was not a continuous fountain of one-liners. He would push us and push us and push us until we were at the brink of meltdown. Then he would stand back and laugh and get us to laugh along with him. The indignities of the day seemed to wash right off our backs, and we felt restored.

Drill Sergeant Morning took his job very seriously, but he did not take *himself* very seriously, and he certainly knew the value of the phrase, "Lighten Up!"

CELEBRATE!
CELEBRATE!
Dance to the Music!

Every soul is a melody which needs renewing.

Stéphane Mallarmé, French poet

If laughter is magic, music and dance are power. The ancients knew this. They would worship with music and dance. The Psalms of the Old Testament are examples. College fight songs, marching songs, ballads, love songs, and satirical songs—they all have immense power to move the soul. Hollywood knows this. Have you ever watched a movie scene where the musical score has been removed? The music produces so much power that the challenge for a musical director is to be sure that it doesn't overpower the actors!

The PhB can use the power of music to enrich the soul.

Music can serve as a reflection of the soul's current state, be it mourning or merriment. It serves as a release valve for the soul. After all, it's not the emotion that can harm us, but the resistance to and the bottling up of emotion that can be injurious to the soul. Without a proper release, emotions can build up until they explode with the force of a psychological Mount St. Helens.

The PhB knows the value of celebration and looks for any and every reason to celebrate. A sunny day? A happy feeling? Perhaps the idea that things could always be worse? A grateful awareness of what we do have, meager as it may be?—all of these are reasons for celebration. For some people the pleasure of friendship is cause for celebration.

Music and dance can enhance the experience. Music can work the emotions, and dance can work the endorphins! It can be observed throughout the world, in both modern and traditional cultures, that it's not the quality level of the performance, but the energy of the celebration that counts. If you're neither singer nor dancer, don't let that stop you. It's joy that the PhB is after, not production value!

What can YOU do?

✓ Listen to all kinds of music to see what moves your soul.

✓ Attend live theatrical events and be aware of how music and movement are used in the show.

✓ Associate music with life events.

✓ Listen for the music of another person's life.

Listening for extra credit

➥ *Les Miserables,* Original Broadway cast

➥ *Man of La Mancha,* Original Broadway cast

➥ *Come Away with Me,* Nora Jones

➥ *The Hallelujah Chorus* from Handel's *Messiah*

*Nothing makes you more tolerant of
a neighbor's noisy party than being there.*

Franklin P. Adams, humorist

Commentary

There is not much to add when it comes to music and dance. They speak for themselves. I would just urge you to use them.

It's true that celebrations should be thoughtful, but there is a certain spark that comes from spontaneity that's lost when celebration becomes routine. Perhaps the deadliest form of sabotage that celebration can be subject to is the specter of *guidelines*, the plastic memo that comes from somewhere on high and says something like,

> While we encourage employee expression of appreciation for jobs well done or birthday celebrations, we nonetheless feel it important to establish suitable guidelines for any activities of such a nature that occur on company property and/or company time. Therefore the following guidelines shall take effect...blah, blah, blah.

Oh, for heaven's sake, lighten up! If you're worried that celebrations at your organization are apt to get out of hand, a little leadership should be able to solve that minor problem. If your corporate counsel insists that this memo is necessary, at least write it with some enthusiasm and care, send it once, bury it in the legal file, then have a raucous celebration about *that!*

HELP
Others

*It is expressly at those times when we feel needy
that we will benefit the most from giving.*

—Ruth Ross

The PhB knows that if you want to help yourself, seek out and help others.

- Helping others takes your mind off *your* problems.
- Helping others puts your problems into perspective.
- Helping others is loving your neighbor.
- Helping others just plain feels good!

Karl Menninger was a renowned psychiatrist and one of the founders of the world famous Menninger Clinic in Kansas. Obviously, he was steeped in the ways of psychiatry, but he was also a first class PhB. Psychiatry was not the only answer to every question.

One day, after he had completed one of his lectures, a member of the audience asked him what someone should do if they felt depression coming on. The audience expected him to say, go to a psychiatrist, but instead he responded, "Leave your house, go across the tracks, find someone who needs help and help that person."

Expert help has a vital place in our society, but there is nothing quite so powerful as the simple act of one human being helping another in distress. Although cash contributions are needed and worthy, they do not substitute for actually coming to the aid of someone in need. It is the act of helping that has such a powerful effect.

It is the act of helping that allows you to truly love your neighbor *and yourself.*

What can YOU do?

✓ Make a conscious effort to help people in ways large and small.

✓ Do not expect anything in return.

✓ Do not let status or rank inhibit the desire to be helpful.

✓ Enjoy the experience!

Reading for extra credit

☞ *The Gift of the Magi*, O. Henry

☞ *Meaning—The Secret of Being Alive*, Cliff Havener

Strange as it may seem, life becomes serene
and enjoyable precisely when selfish pleasures
and personal success are no longer the guiding goals.

—Mihaly Csikszentmihalyi, psychologist

Commentary

It is ironic that in helping another you are surely helping yourself. No amount of cash, no attainment of higher rank, no vast number of accumulated material things—nothing else compares to the uplift and spark you receive by simply helping a fellow human being.

The gift does not have to be large to be effective.

In high school, I was on my way to a Christmas event. It was a breezy, snowy evening, so driving took some concentration. You wouldn't want to be taking a walk in the weather we were having that night.

I happened upon a car with a flat tire. As I drove by, I saw a man at the wheel of a car chock full of family—Grandpa and Grandma, wife, and three children—all dressed for some event they were on their way to. They looked less than thrilled to be stuck on the road in inclement weather, and it was obvious they had been there for more than a minute or two. Their dark skin and foreign look probably was not inviting to motorists passing by.

My practical sense was prodding me to drive on, but I couldn't get the helpless looks I had seen out of my mind. I turned around, went back, and pulled up behind them.

As I approached the window, I could see that there was a certain amount of hesitation written on the driver's face. Reluctantly, he rolled down the window. When he heard my offer to help him change his tire, his face broke into a warm smile.

I discovered that he had shut off their engine to save the little gas they had, so the car was very cold. Violating all common sense, I piled Grandpa and Grandma, his wife and kids into my car, which was running and quite toasty. Papa and I set about to change the tire in the snow and cold. Papa proved to be of little mechanical assistance, however, so I pushed him into my car too. I should clarify something—when I write "my car", that is not entirely accurate. It was my *father's* car I was driving that night.

I must admit I half expected to see my father's car pull away without me. I was rehearsing my defense while attacking the faulty tire, but then I thought what the heck. It's Christmas!

The tire was changed. My father's car stayed put. The family trekked back to their own car, and as we wished each other a Merry Christmas, Papa's eyes got a trifle moist, and he said, "Thank you, my friend, thank you!"

Best Christmas present I ever got.

What's really exciting, though, is the lift I get any time I think of that man and his family.

I helped him once.

The memory of his simple gratitude has helped me many, many times during the intervening 42 years.

If you were a business analyst, who would you say benefited the most from that deal?

Like so many other things that one can do to be a PhB, helping others is time-consuming and highly inefficient. No doubt it's more time-effective to make a donation. But donations can't clasp your hand in friendship or give voice to emotion.

Only human contact can do that.

STAND BY
Your Word

*One stumble is enough to deface
the character of an honorable life.*

—L. Estrange

The PhB knows that a person's word is the most important foundation upon which to build a relationship.

More friendships, business opportunities, and self-improvement benefits have been lost because a person's word was not kept than for any other reason.

Say what you mean and mean what you say. Then follow through.

Keeping one's word is the brick and mortar of success. And it's an ongoing, continuous process that must be carefully adhered to and treasured. It is one of life's more bizarre truths that it takes a very long time to establish that one's word is good, but only one slip to lose all credibility.

It is also ironic that the keeping of one's word is rarely heralded and publicized. It's something that people come to expect. But when one fails to do so, the publicity is sudden and overwhelming.

Keeping your word is something you do for yourself. Your personal integrity is of enormous value to you in how you deal with others. It is a nice by-product of personal integrity that after *years* of displaying it, someone may come up to you and thank you for it.

What can YOU do?

✓ Tell the truth as you know it.

✓ If you say you will, make sure you do!

✓ State your position straightforwardly and simply, without embellishment.

✓ Fully understand the sometimes high cost of standing by your word and pay it.

Reading for extra credit

✎ *Leadership in Times of Stress and Change,* Harry L. Woodward, Ph.D. and Mark J. Tager, M.D.

✎ *Horton Hears a Who,* Dr. Suess

✎ *Land of the Giants,* Don Larson

Whenever you do a thing,
act as if all the world were watching.

—Thomas Jefferson

Commentary

One might have the inclination to lump this section with the section on integrity. Indeed, they're almost inseparable. A person with integrity will keep his or her word.

It seems to me, however, that the simple act of keeping one's word is perhaps the first step toward real integrity. The more often you keep your word, the more you deposit to your integrity bank. At some point in the future (more than likely the distant future) your integrity bank account will serve you well.

Keeping one's word should be such a simple act, but often it is not.

Simple manners suggest that if you make a promise, you keep a promise. Keeping your word is a matter of habit. The more you practice it, the more it becomes a part of you.

Developing this habit is important because there will come a time when keeping your word will be a challenge.

Why?

It may cost you substantial amounts of money. It may prove to be "socially embarrassing." Some people will call you a damn fool for doing it! It may cost you a long-established relationship. Of course, a relationship that cannot withstand integrity is probably best ended. The point is that unless you have forged a pattern of behavior for yourself by keeping your word, it might well be very difficult to do so when it is most needed.

In the days of the moon shots, the National Aeronautical and Space Administration (NASA) was successful in its missions because the astronauts were required to practice their flight plans in simulators over and over again. They also tried to anticipate unexpected events and practiced recognizing and responding to them. By the time the actual launch date arrived, the astronaut crews and ground teams had been to the moon and back hundreds of times by way of the simulator.

In the case of Apollo 13, an oxygen cell exploded on the outbound journey toward the moon. The three-man crew was in desperate straits as they were speeding *away* from their home planet through an airless frozen void in a badly damaged spacecraft. Because they and the ground crews had trained and practiced endlessly for the mission, they were able to respond to an emergency that had not been anticipated.

You must keep in mind that the computers NASA was using in those days had less power than the standard desktop anyone can buy today, so it wasn't just a quick change of variables loaded into a computer program that would then generate a solution. In the case of Apollo 13, much of the computation was done manually on slide rules, and the solution that was finally cobbled together had been sketched out on paper, and made use of the parts and materials on hand in the spacecraft itself.

Because of the habits they had acquired during all those hours in simulation, each person knew exactly what was available, and could put together a radically modified, yet workable, flight plan that gave the astronauts a chance to return to Earth safely. Had they *not* cultivated these habits, they wouldn't have known where to begin in their efforts to come up with a successful solution to their dilemma.

Keeping your word is a similar habit-forming discipline that will serve you well when the going becomes difficult and hazardous.

Start *today* making a habit of keeping your word in matters both large and small.

LOVE
Yourself

Love is a medicine for the sickness of the world;
a prescription often given, too rarely taken.

—Karl A. Menninger, psychiatrist

Do the best you can with what you've got where you are.

—George Washington Carver

Love of one's self is of basic importance to the act of loving another. If one is not entirely comfortable with his or her own way of being—indeed, if one actually experiences a degree of self-loathing, then loving others fully is not possible.

If you are comfortable in your own skin, then you have vast resources of love and energy to give to someone else.

So begin each day looking at your face in the mirror and apply the first eight chapters of this book to the person you see there. What does this person possess? Does this person value others? Does this person have integrity? Does this person choose to have a positive outlook on life? Does this person understand and practice humility? Does this person know how to laugh, celebrate, and help others? Does this person's word have meaning at all times in every situation on any day?

If this is not the case in one or more of these attributes of the Professional Human Being, then the first person to benefit should be that person in the mirror. If you're willing to look at yourself with brutal honestly and put forth the tremendous effort required to be the best human being you can be, *then you are deserving of the title, PhB.*

What can YOU do?

✓ No negative self talk.

✓ Give yourself a break.

✓ You alone are responsible for your happiness.

Reading for extra credit

✎ *Loving What Is,* Byron Katie with Stephen Mitchell

*For what other dungeon is so dark as one's own heart!
What jailer so inexorable as one's self!*

—Nathaniel Hawthorne

Commentary

We all know people who love themselves much too much. If you suspect you are one of these, I suggest you return to the lesson on humility, read it again thoroughly, and be sure to do *all* the homework.

This commentary is directed to those gentle souls who are truly humble or at least very timid.

You are a good person who likes people and doesn't hesitate to do good things for them when you can. You are in awe of those around you who can perform so well. You are often amazed at how people you're pretty sure have less talent than you do seem to be doing better and being promoted faster or receiving more recognition. Sometimes you wonder why the forces of the universe seem to have chosen you for unwanted martyrdom. You try and try and try, but the world just doesn't seem to give a rip. So you quietly go about your life, trying to do the right thing, always questioning yourself, always harboring just a bit of envy and resentment, and waiting for your turn in the sun.

Do you recognize yourself in the above description or any part of it? If you're honest enough with yourself to admit it, you probably have felt at least some, if not all of these feelings, perhaps on a daily basis.

Take heart! You are not alone. Many, *many* people have felt the way you do.

There's just one catch, though. No, actually, there are two.

- These negative feelings are not good for you, and
- *You don't need to feel this way.*

Let me repeat something I wrote at the beginning of the first lesson.

> You are absolutely unique. In the history of the world there has never been another you. And in the future, there never will be another you.

Just as the late Herb Brooks told his U.S. Hockey team before the game with the mighty Russians in the 1980 Olympics—the "Miracle on Ice"—I will tell you,

"You have a *right* to be here."

You do!

But if you're waiting around for someone to recognize that right or to hand it to you in some ceremonial fashion, you will be disappointed.

Your happiness is up to you. The first best thing you can do for yourself is to lighten up a little. Stop being your own harshest critic.

You have a *right* to be here.

It took me many years to understand this idea. And it's important to understand it.

You say you love your fellow human beings, but you are selfless. I will tell you that unless you love yourself as well, you can't know what it is to truly love another.

You see, if you continue to concentrate on all your own flaws, you will also see them quite a bit more readily in other people. In fact, without meaning to at all, you may become quite self-righteous. I know, because I have.

So when you're showing compassion and love for your neighbor be sure to include some for yourself.

You have a *right* to be here.

"Be yourself; no base imitator of another, but your best self.
There is something which you can do better than another.
Listen to the inward voice and bravely obey that. Do the things
at which you are great, not what you were never made for."

—Ralph Waldo Emerson

FIND YOUR PURPOSE AND LIVE!

The meaning of our existence is not invented by ourselves, but rather detected.

—Viktor Frankl

I f you think that life is just chaos with no rhyme, reason, or meaning to it at all, you might be tempted to skip this chapter.

If you do *not* believe that life is just a permanent state of chaos, then you have probably wondered just why you exist. What should I be doing with my life? What is the ultimate purpose of my existence?

The PhB continually asks these questions. It's a never-ending search for meaning in one's life.

If you're lucky, you may find your purpose early in life and have what seems like unlimited time to pursue it. However, consider the idea that most people search a lifetime to discover their purpose. More confusing is the idea that purpose may change as life evolves. What your purpose was in your 30s may have nothing in common with the purpose you pursue in your 50s. The PhB is open to such changes.

Also, consider that the purpose you seek may not be the purpose that seeks you. Events unfold in your life that may have a profound effect on your perception of what is important to you. The purpose you end up with may not be one that you ever considered or even wanted.

Also remember that your purpose is for you alone. Your purpose is not my purpose.

The PhB knows that deep contemplation is essential for discovering the deep purpose in one's life and that the search for purpose is ongoing.

So the PhB doesn't become discouraged by the search, as endless as it may appear while in the middle of it. The PhB knows that the failures encountered in the search eliminate those things that do not fit. And knowing that purpose may change along the way, the PhB is keenly aware that the search is ongoing and is excited about the new possibilities that it presents.

What Can YOU do?

✓ Actively search for your purpose.

✓ Be open to the idea that your purpose may find you!

✓ When your intuition urges you in a direction, follow it.

Reading for extra credit

☞ *Answering Your Call—A Guide to Living Your Deepest Purpose*, John P. Schuster

☞ *The Power of Purpose—Creating Meaning in Your Life and Work*, Richard J. Leider

☞ *Finding Flow—The Psychology of Engagement with Everyday Life*, Mihaly Csikszentmihalyi

☞ *Second Innocence—Rediscovering Joy and Wonder*, John Izzo

People like you and I, though mortal of course
like everyone else, do not grow old no matter how long we live…
[We] never cease to stand like curious children before
the great mystery into which we were born.

—Albert Einstein

How different our lives are when we really know what is deeply
important to us, and keeping that picture in mind, we manage
ourselves each day to be and to do what really matters most.

—Stephen Covey

Commentary

If you accept the notion that you are unique—that no one like you has ever existed before or will ever exist again—then the notion of purpose in your life is not a difficult one to contemplate.

Each person has certain talents and gifts they have been blessed with. Some are destined to accomplish things on a scale grand enough to be noted in history books. Most of us, however, will be operating on a smaller scale, one that will never be noticed by anyone but those we touch in our daily lives. That's OK.

Almost everyone I've met has asked themselves if there is purpose to life. And if there is purpose to life, then what is my unique purpose?

I wish there were some concrete guidance I could give to answer that question, but alas, there is not.

It's probably just as well, because it's been my experience, and that of many of the people I come in contact with, that finding one's purpose in life is an individual journey, and one that's vastly different for each of us.

One of my favorite stories is about a young Italian violinist who was born in the mid 1600s. His passion was the violin, and he studied and practiced the violin with one goal in mind—to become the world's best violinist.

Surely, this was his destiny. Surely, this was his reason to live, his purpose. His love of the instrument was unbounded, and his passion was intense.

But one day he realized that despite his passion, despite his very best effort and dedication, he lacked the talent needed to become one of the most highly regarded musicians. It was absolutely devastating to him to understand that he could not fulfill his dream.

Though he would not attain his first goal, he retained a love for the instrument. He began to study violin construction, woods, finishes, and fingerboards. If he couldn't *be* the best violinist in the world, then he would *build* the best violins in the world.

His name was Antonio Stradivarius, and his violins are considered to be the finest ever constructed, even today. Many of the violins Stradivarius crafted are still in existence, and still widely used by professionals almost 300 years after his death.

Passion for something does not in and of itself mean that you have discovered purpose.

Sometimes purpose discovers you.

Many a great cause had its roots in a totally unexpected event. Candy Lightner, the woman who founded Mothers Against Drunk Driving (MADD) lost a child in a traffic accident involving a drunk driver. Rather than simply mourn her loss, she decided to do something to prevent it from happening again.

Is this a purpose that she would willingly have chosen? Of course not! But it's a purpose, nonetheless.

I speak to audiences large and small across the country. I speak because I love to do it and because I have a story to tell that often helps folks to live with a new view, new excitement, and a new sense of fulfillment.

I sometimes regret that it took me a good 50 years to find and embrace my own purpose!

Yet, when I really think about it, I'm pretty sure I could not have hurried the process along. I believe I had to experience what I did, struggle the way I did, *at the pace I did,* so as to make me effective at what I do today. Perhaps the experience of my longer journey can help shorten yours.

A purpose can also be a temporary phenomenon.

I have known two people who have gone to prison. One has been one of my very closest friends for over 40 years. His story appears in the Appendix. My experience with the other, whom I did not know so well, will serve as an example of what I mean about temporary purpose.

Before this man was sent to prison, I really didn't like him very much. He was aggressive, arrogant, intimidating, and otherwise quite unappealing to me.

Then I heard him talk about his faith in a public forum. He said he was a work in progress, and he stunned the audience by telling them (with great difficulty) that he was going to prison. In listening to his story, I realized I had never known him on a deeper level—what his background was like (less than perfect) or what drove him to be the way he was.

His father was a violent alcoholic. Once, he very nearly killed his father because he stepped in to stop the man from beating his mother in an alcoholic rage. He learned to rely entirely upon himself. His youthful understanding of life led him to believe that the harder he drove himself, the more he would succeed. This idea was reinforced when he won a basketball scholarship to college. After graduating from college, obtaining a job as a commission-based investment broker was a natural progression for him. He proved himself quickly and was managing an entire office at a young age. Eventually, he started a money management firm that gave him authority over other people's assets.

Over the years of his personal success, he had become quite arrogant about his abilities and was sure *he* knew what was best for the clients. This arrogance resulted in his placing funds in totally inappropriate investments for the risk levels of his customers. When they lost money and his fees dropped precipitously, he "borrowed" from one of his clients without their knowledge in order to support his lavish life style.

He was caught.

He was about to put a gun to his head when he decided to call a friend. The friend was a man of great faith. He gently brought the investment manager back to his senses and literally saved his life.

He kept the audience mesmerized for 45 minutes, and when he sat down, there was dead silence as people contemplated what they had just heard.

I was strongly compelled to write to him during his prison term. I enjoyed the weekly ritual of composing a letter to him and trying to decide what else to send him. He wrote back on a fairly regular basis, and for the 15 months of his term we had a wonderful relationship. After he was released, I met with him a couple of times, and he even invited me to his wedding.

Since the wedding I have had almost no contact with the man. At first I fretted about it, thinking that maybe I was letting him down or something. But the reality was that we had simply drifted away from one another.

I had been compelled to a definite purpose during his prison term, but he was now quite capable of moving on under his own auspices. The purpose was no longer valid, so we let it go.

One last thought about purpose:

The journey toward purpose is just as important as discovering purpose itself. I find it quite astonishing that life seems to provide you with exactly what you need at the moment you need it. It may not be what you *want* at that moment, mind you, but there it is. If you keep yourself open to the possibilities and on the lookout for purpose, I have no doubt you will find it.

Or it will find you.

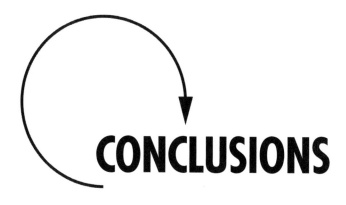

CONCLUSIONS

Perhaps we were placed on this planet for something more profound than feeding and caring for "The System." Perhaps an appreciation of ourselves and other human beings could contribute mightily to changing and improving The System.

Paraphrasing an ancient book, "What good does it do a person to gain the whole world, but lose his or her humanity in the process?"

It is up to you to be a human being. No one else can do it for you. And if you weren't quite sure how to go about it, now you have a point of departure in this book.

Today is an excellent day to begin the journey!

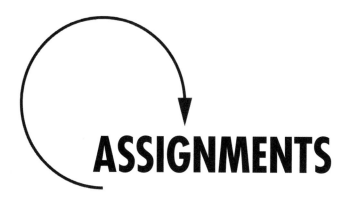

ASSIGNMENTS

1. Read one chapter of this book per week until each chapter is second nature to you.

2. Keep a personal journal and use it to make notes daily on what you did well and what you did not do well as a human being. Also use it for observations, random thoughts, and recording emotions and results.

3. Once a month take an hour to read your journal, contemplate its messages, and plan for the next month.

4. Once a quarter, but no less than once a year, find a retreat and go there for a minimum of two days to contemplate and meditate about yourself and others, about your performance as a human being, about the purpose of your life, and whether you have been fulfilling that purpose. If you have such a belief, get in touch with your creator and have active discussions with your creator about life, humanity, and purpose. At the conclusion of the retreat, write down what you've learned, discovered, been made privy to, and what your plan is to use what you've learned.

5. Put your plan in a place where you can look at it every day of the year to remind yourself of the solemn vows you made, and to make it an integral part of your everyday direction.

6. If you experience trouble with any of the steps laid out above, seriously consider engaging the services of a coach to help guide you through the process. Coaches might be described as something like professional friends—they have only your best interests at heart. They don't much care about how you are perceived by your organization, yet they are an objective sounding board for you, and they know the importance of absolute confidentiality.

7. THEN SMILE AND ENJOY THE MOMENT!

Journaling is very Important.

Keep this in mind about journaling:

* THIS JOURNAL IS FOR YOU ALONE.
* It will not be graded for structure or content.
* If you like bullet points, use them.
* If you like to write, write as much as you want.
* Do it regularly.

The key to journaling is to be absolutely honest in your entries, no matter what the subject, emotion, or thought you're recording. Whether bullet points or essays (or both, separately and together), you must record your truest, most honest expressions.

If you're true to yourself, look at all you can do:

* Journaling gives you a reference point for yourself. You'll be amazed at some of the things you can accomplish just by writing them down and reviewing them. Sometimes they happen almost by themselves.

* You will also be fascinated by your own sound ideas and misconceptions.

* You'll be able to chart progress and changes in thinking and direction.

* You can get a sense of where you are today, where you want to go in the future, and what progress you are making.

The last word of advice I have on journaling is to do it regularly! "Regularly" for you might be daily, weekly, or monthly. Anything longer than monthly is self-defeating. I would recommend at least bi-weekly or more often.

APPENDIX
REAL STORIES ABOUT REAL PhBs

Some heroes carry a gun and show bravery on the battlefield.

Some heroes carry, bounce, or shoot a ball in the sports world.

*Some heroes do the tough jobs that must be done without
fanfare or acknowledgment. Those, perhaps,
are the greatest heroes of them all.***

** I heard this on a radio show. I came in on the tail end of the conversation,
so I can't tell you who said it or in what context. I *do* know that it is true and
meaningful for the people you meet in these stories of real PhBs.

These are true stories about everyday people that I know personally. Most of them are good friends who have shown me their inner selves and who have allowed me to share their stories with you.

Bruce

I got to know Bruce through my breakfast club. The club meets every Wednesday morning throughout the year, and the basic criteria for membership is good fellowship—a bunch of guys who like to get together, listen to speakers, and enjoy each other's company.

Over the course of the last 25 years we have slowly gotten to know each other better.

We ended up in the same Bible study group with several other "reprobates" from the breakfast club. It was here that Bruce revealed the depth of his intellect and his thoughtful contemplation of what it means to be spiritual in a secular world.

He has asked probing questions of himself and of others. He has read many books of spirituality and has shared his findings with the group.

He doesn't claim to be better than other people, but he does adhere to his own high standards. For a variety of reasons he chose those standards for himself, and his goal has been to live up to them to the best of his ability.

This was never more evident than when he decided to exit the financial services business. His career had spanned almost 40 years. He sold his business to a large corporation, worked for them as an equal partner for eight years, and then decided that it was time to move on.

He could have done what many a business person has done, that is, take the money and run. But he chose to stay fully committed to his clients and employees so that, as he said, "It was done the right way." He put in many hours of extra work and made an enormous emotional investment because he thought it was "the right thing to do."

He felt an obligation to the acquiring firm to present them with the strongest possible relationship with his clients that he could produce so that retention was a genuine possibility when he left.

He felt an even larger obligation to his clients and employees to make sure the transition was as smooth as possible.

When tough situations arose, he could have passed them on to somebody else. After all, he had his money, and he had fulfilled the letter of his agreement.

However, his personal standards compelled him to follow through instead of walking away. "A lot of my success," he said, "came about from a commitment to duty."

I sat down with Bruce one day, and during an hour's worth of conversation, he revealed more about what drives him, what makes him tick, why he lives his life the way he does.

He used several words a number of times—intuition, choice, spirituality, and divine spark.

"Over the years I've learned to trust my intuition, my instinct for things. I know when it's time to make a change. I know what's right and what I have to do."

Was there a particular moment when he *knew* the way he would live?

"No," he said. "Actually it evolved over time. Oh, I knew that my approach to life was in some way a conscious reaction to watching those of the previous generation, and how they lived their lives. I gradually became committed to providing the best customer service I could. My career was focused on my customers, so much so that I think maybe I let some opportunities pass me by. I can't point to a moment of epiphany where I had some sudden flash of insight. I just kept working at it as my career unfolded."

Given his keen interest in the subject, has spirituality played a part in the pattern of his life?

"Yes, but not in the way you might expect. I don't regularly throw things out to God and blindly accept what comes back to me. I study a situation or a challenge very closely and try to figure out all the possible scenarios that might result from decisions and actions I can take. As I said, I rely heavily on my intuition to guide me. I do believe that there is a divine spark in my intuition. At some point in life you learn to trust that intuition completely. There is energy in the universe that is available to anyone in that sixth sense that we have if we choose to access it. It has a distinctly protective spiritual tone to it.

"Also, I've learned to trust the fact that I don't have to control everything to realize a good outcome. I don't allow myself to become attached to a particular outcome. In that sense I'm willing to present different scenarios to the universe and trust in the one that eventually evolves. I'm open to other possibilities.

"By the way, that energy has shown up in many religious figures throughout history. I choose to draw on them all."

Like most PhBs Bruce has made conscious choices as to what he does, how he acts, and what standards he maintains. He also acknowledges that there are other forces at work in his life—the energy available to him through his intuition, for example—and these forces can be most helpful to him when he chooses to access them.

He has a ready smile and an insatiable curiosity, and he treats people with dignity because "it's the right thing to do."

Theresa

Theresa is a brand-new pal of mine. She is the stepdaughter of a friend who's a member in that breakfast club I mentioned earlier. Her father has the patience of Job when he plays golf with me. He gives me tips, lines me up, and never winces when my shot goes awry.

One day at breakfast he told me about Theresa. How we got on the subject I do not recall, but when he finished telling me about her, I knew I had to get to know her and include her story.

She is 21 years old as this is written.

She smiles easily and has an infectious giggle.

She is wise well beyond her years.

She has a faith, formed in a crucible, that most of us take a lifetime to develop and assert.

She has an appeal about her that is absolutely lovely, but she is as tough as nails.

It would be easy to overlook her because of her small stature, but it would be a major mistake to do so for she has limitless goodwill to share with those around her.

She is majoring in psychology, and although she is unsure of exactly what she will do when she graduates, she thinks that some sort of counseling will be involved. "I know I have a purpose for my life. I just need to discover exactly what it is. After everything I've been through, I just don't believe that things happen for no reason at all."

You see, Theresa was born with something called Turner Syndrome. It's a genetic anomaly where one chromosome (one of the X chromosomes) has been dropped from her genetic code. It is an exclusively a female condition. Males have an X and a Y chromosome. Females have two X chromosomes. The reason there are no males with Turner Syndrome is that a Y chromosome cannot exist without an X chromosome. Therefore male babies cannot survive the missing X chromosome. However, an X chromosome *can* exist alone in the female.

Most women with Turner Syndrome may have one or two complications to deal with, but in rare cases virtually all the complications are in evidence.

Theresa is one of those rare cases.

What follows is a list of the twenty operations she has endured in her young life:

- coarctation of the aorta
- pericardial effusion (fluid around the heart)
- reconstructive chest wall surgery
- insertion of rods in her back to correct scoliosis
- combination pectus surgery
- four surgeries to have sets of tubes put in her ears
- four surgeries to repair a lesion on her head that wouldn't grow hair
- four reconstructive ear surgeries
- removal of tonsils
- removal of adenoids
- repair of webbed neck
- removal of wisdom teeth (necessary to avoid complications with her heart)

Theresa describes her extraordinary childhood as "somewhat trying"! Her classmates at school would tease her because she was different. She says, "They didn't know any better. They are trying to understand the world around them, and when something or someone is different, it just throws things off. Oh, it still hurt me—a lot. But then one day my mother gave me a growth hormone shot in front of the entire class, and that seemed to do the trick. Now they understood that being different was not something I could help, and it also helped them learn something more about me."

Subsequently, she has given talks about Turner Syndrome to her fellow students to help them understand and break through the wall of ignorance that separates them.

Was there ever a time when she didn't feel she could face going to school? "Only once," she says. "We moved just before I started the tenth grade. I had to face going to a new school—which is difficult enough—but also the education of new class-mates as to what it's like to be me had to begin again. Fortunately, I made two friends very quickly. Yes, there were a couple of kids that just had to make fun of me, but I ignored them."

Theresa talks about her family and how their support helped her grow and survive a seemingly endless series of operations and doctor visits. Her mother—especially her mother—was always encouraging her and telling her that there wasn't any-thing she couldn't do if she wanted to. (Please see the next story)

And she adores her stepfather. "Oh, he's just great!" she says. "I love him."

Of her own father she says very little. "I don't have a rela-tionship with him," she says, and that pretty much covers the subject.

She's a straight talker and a truth teller. She speaks freely about herself, her family, her friends, and her faith.

And she is a welcome bright light in our world.

Mary Jo and Dave

Originally, I had thought I would tell only Theresa's story, but her eloquence and her obviously affection and appreciation for her mother and stepfather led me to want to hear their story as well.

Mary Jo was 23 when she had Theresa. Her first daughter was two-and-a-half years old. The nurses took the newly born Theresa out of the delivery room, and Mary Jo didn't see her that night. The next day, the doctor came into her room with a photocopy of two pages from a medical book. The two pages described Turner Syndrome. The doctor's words were, "It looks like you have a mentally retarded dwarf on your hands."

Her husband was a manic-depressive alcoholic so there was no help or support to be had there.

Mary Jo went home only to have her sutures burst (the birth was Caesarean). She was resutured and told to return in one week to have them checked. She asked to bring Theresa in at the same time, since the baby would be ready for her two-week checkup.

At home Theresa was having a difficult time. She would drink only a quarter of an ounce of milk. Then she would projectile vomit it back up.

When they arrived at the doctor's office for the checkup, the medical team realized that Theresa was on the verge of cardiac arrest. She was taken to Children's Hospital where they tried to take care of her with drug therapy. But a few days later Theresa had her first operation—open heart surgery as a three-week-old!

The medical staff said to Mary Jo, "That is one tough little girl you have there," and that is when the mother became empowered by her daughter. "I just had to help her. I had to! She became my inspiration. She is the one who kept me going, who supported me. People want to praise me and tell me how impressed they are at how I handled everything with Theresa, but she is the one who was impressive. She has been such a gift to me." With eyes glistening and voice choking, Mary Jo apologizes for how emotional she gets when she speaks of her daughter.

After a third daughter was born, the marriage finally ended, and Mary Jo was on her own. Theresa's medical problems and surgical procedures virtually bankrupted her. She worked four jobs and became adept at finding out-of-the-way pharmacies in distant towns where she could have prescriptions filled and paid for with checks that needed a long float so she could earn enough money to deposit in the account before they finally cleared.

Her oldest daughter earned money for the family as well. Her brother worked weekends and gave the extra cash to the family.

"It wasn't a matter of pride. I had to survive! I was in the church basement looking for clothes and food."

Amazingly enough, Mary Jo was not angry or bitter about the lot she had been given. "No, I didn't get mad at God or ask why me? Frankly, I was too busy trying to keep my family intact and taking care of Theresa to be mad. The only time I would get angry was when I didn't have enough money to take care of Theresa. Why should she be deprived of what she needed? That isn't fair! But mostly I was grateful for friends and family and the kind charity of others who unhesitatingly helped me. It's difficult to be angry where love abounds."

For ten years Mary Jo carried on alone with her girls.

Then she met Dave.

Dave had been married once before and had grown sons. As he puts it, "I had been dating 'power women'—women who were professionals or executives or company owners. But I wasn't fulfilled by them. There was something lacking. I wrote down the 20 attributes I really wanted from a relationship with a woman, and none of them had anything to do with power, wealth, or status. Then I met Mary Jo.

"We were supposed to see the movie *Titanic* but it was sold out, so we ended up going to a restaurant for about three hours. We talked and talked and talked. When I got home, I thought of Mary Jo, and I checked off 19 of the 20 attributes on my list, and now I've checked off all 20!"

Dave had some issues about getting together with Mary Jo— three of them, in fact. "My sons were grown, and I had never had daughters. I have to be honest about it. The daughters were something to think about, and yes, Theresa's problems gave me pause as well."

Dave's love for Mary Jo overcame any lingering hesitation, and now there were new challenges.

"Melissa, the oldest, was not happy about my arrival for a long time. You have to realize that she had been a co-parent with Mary Jo for most of her life. With my presence she lost her status as co-parent and became one of the kids again. This was a difficult transition for her. Theresa accepted me right away, and I was completely captivated by her. Andrea, the youngest, was OK with me, too—after awhile.

"Hey, it's different with girls! Theresa invited me to a father/ daughter dance at her school. It happened to be on a night of the Final Four NCAA basketball championships, and if you know me, well, that is sacred time. But how could I say no to her? So I went to this dance, and I saw how all the dads were with their daughters. Their eyes were positively glowing, and they couldn't have prouder of them. I have always been proud of my sons, but my eyes didn't glow, you know?

"Well, I went to the same dance with her the next year, and I told her that I thought I let her down last year because this glowing-eye thing was new to me. 'But *this* year,' I said, 'my eyes can glow with the best of them.'"

Dave's eyes can glisten pretty well these days too.

If you listen to Mary Jo and Dave tell their stories, you are struck by how open and honest they are. They don't brag, but they don't hold back the truth either. They don't minimize the challenges they have faced together.

Dave and Mary Jo aren't Superman and Superwoman. They're ordinary people with the ability to look outside themselves and appreciate what life, in all its various guises, can bring them. They are, beyond all doubt, PhBs.

Steve

Steve's story is a little bit different. He was a PhB. Then he wasn't, and now he is again.

Steve has been one of my best friends for 40 years, ever since high school. He was a new kid from Chicago who came into our class as a sophomore. He was friendly, smart, athletic, and very strong.

He went on to become a lawyer and started his own law firm. It seemed there wasn't anything he couldn't do when he set his mind to it.

Somewhere in his success he lost his humility. The loss was not sudden. It was like a pinprick leak in a tank—barely perceptible but continuous. He became habitually late to his appointments and didn't seem to have much time for his friends. When he was with you, he was still the same friendly soul you had always known, but he wasn't with you much.

Steve decided that he wanted to be a businessman, so he quit his law firm and was hired to run a fledgling medical company. That was when things really unraveled for him.

"I started living 'the good life,'" he says. I had control of the finances of the company, I could make business trips to New York or wherever I wanted whenever I wanted. I was in charge.

"But I realize, looking back on it now, I was also living against all the values I had grown up with. Not wanting to admit that to myself, and wanting some protection from facing up to the facts, I drank."

Steve became an alcoholic.

The insidiousness of alcoholism goes beyond the episodes of getting blotto. Even when sober, the alcoholic does things that defy common sense and decency.

He had been promised stock in the company he was running, but the owner decided not to follow through on that promise, so Steve issued himself the stock he thought he rightly deserved, and pledged it as collateral for a bank loan. He also continued an emerging pattern of lies in just about every phase of his life.

He got divorced, fired from his job, investigated by the bar association, and eventually indicted for the improper stock issuance.

"One weekend I was sitting in my crummy little apartment, preparing to face a grand jury proceeding the next Monday. I knew that the divorce deposition I had given the year before would be part of the procedure, so I had to review it.

"As I read the deposition, I wondered who this monster was who had given it. And I knew it was me. It was my first conscious realization of the man I had become, and I was devastated.

"I called a friend of mine and asked him to come over. I really needed to talk to someone. My friend convinced me I needed to be tested for chemical dependency, so I went that Monday after the grand jury proceedings. Long story short, I needed treatment.

"Then things got worse."

Steve was convicted and sentenced to prison for fifteen months. "My life was over," he says quietly. "I was 45 years old, no money, no family, and going to prison. Who would ever talk to me again? I truly felt my life was over."

Steve reported to the prison facility and felt utterly alone and frightened. In prison, the inmates are required to have a job. They can request a particular job or else be assigned one if they express no preference. For the first month Steve, having sunk into depression, merely went through the motions.

At the end of that first month, he was sitting on a bench outside on a cold, cloudy, foggy day, and as he says, "From out of nowhere this feeling came to me, this feeling of peace. I *knew* that I was going to be OK. It had been a year almost to the day since I had stopped drinking. I mean, it wasn't like there were golden rays of light from heaven streaming down upon me or anything. I just knew that I'd be OK."

When asked if he thinks this feeling was divinely inspired, he simply says, "Yes."

The very next day, he happened to sit next to an inmate who was getting out. Because of this man's departure, an instructor was needed for the education program. Steve immediately applied for the job and was accepted.

"It was the beginning of my salvation," he says. "I helped teach guys how to write to their wives and children. I helped them get their GED (General Equivalency Degree). I prepared them to pass tests necessary for their release. I taught them everything I could.

"On visiting days, oftentimes one of the wives would come up to me and hug me and whisper to me, 'Thank you. Oh, thank you.' Guys would visit me at my bunk for advice, or to say thank you to me. In eight months, I managed to graduate ten times the number of guys that had graduated in the prior seven years of the program's existence."

He says again, "It was the beginning of my salvation. It taught me the true meaning of service to others. It gave me purpose and fulfillment. And it allowed me to be of service to myself. I got my health back by working out six days a week."

When Steve was released, his son picked him up to take him to the halfway house. "That was really cool. I didn't think anyone would ever want to see me or talk to me again."

He sent his job resume out and as his last position of employment, he listed *prison*. He was referred by a former client (a real PhB) to someone who asked him "tell me the whole story." He was hired and has worked for the man (another PhB) ever since.

He has recently remarried.

Have there been challenges since his recovery? "Oh yes! The biggest challenge was to reestablish relationships with family and friends. There was my sense of shame and guilt, of course, but it was even deeper than that. I remembered all the things I had done to everyone, and I was acutely aware of all the things I'd missed—especially with my children. You can never go back and recapture those times."

Steve's story is quite instructional. It shows us that it takes work and awareness to remain a PhB. Steve was one, and then he wasn't. If not tended carefully, our PhB can slip away. His story also shows us that there is redemption, that *anyone*, no matter where they've been or what they've done, is capable of becoming a PhB again.

I know this is true because my good friend Steve taught it to me.

Remember:

1. Value other People

2. Integrity: Be a Seeker of the Truth, not a Manipulator of Facts

3. Choose a Positive Attitude.

4. Understand and Practice Humility.

5. Be Open.

6. Let Go.

7. Laugh!

8. Celebrate, Celebrate! Dance to the Music!

9. Help Others

10. Stand by Your Word

11. Love Yourself

12. Find Your Purpose and Live!

CONSOLIDATED READING LIST

- Hyrum W. Smith, *What Matters Most—The Power of Living Your Values,* (New York, FIRESIDE, 2001)
- Viktor E. Frankl, *Man's Search for Meaning,* (New York, Beacon Press, 1959)
- Kevin & Jackie Freiberg, Nuts—*Southwest Airlines' Crazy Recipe for Business and Personal Success,* (New York, Broadway Books, 1996)
- Stephen C. Lundin, Harry Paul, and John Christensen, *Fish—A Remarkable Way to Boost Morale and Improve Results,* (New York, Hyperion, 2000)
- Byron Katie with Stephen Mitchell, *Loving What Is—Four questions that cam change your life,* (New York, Harmony Books, 2002)
- Shel Horowitz, *Principled Profit—Marketing that puts people first,* (Northampton, AWM Books, 2003)
- Jim Collins, *Level Five Leadership: The Triumph of Humility and Fierce Resolve,* (Cambridge, Harvard Business School Press, 2004)
- Ken Jennings and John Stahl-Wert, *The Serving Leader: 5 Powerful Actions that will Transform Your Team, Your*

Business, and Your Community (San Fancisco: Berrett-Koehler Publishers, 2003).

- Lenora Billings-Harris, *The Diversity Advantage—A Guide to Making Diversity Work,* Greensboro, Oakhill Press, 1998

- Rosamund Stone Zander, Benjamin Zander, *The Art of Possibility—Transforming Professional and Personal Life,* (Cambridge, Harvard Business School Press, 2000)

- Joseph Jaworski, *Synchronicity—The Inner Path of Leadership,* (San Francisco, Berrett-Koehler Publishers, 1996)

- Cliff Havener, *Meaning—The Secret of Being Alive,* (Edina, Beaver's Pond Press, 1999)

- Dale L. Anderson, Arden Moore, *Never Act Your Age: Play the Happy Childlike Role at Every Age,* (Edina, Beaver's Pond Press, 2002)

- Steve Rizzo, *Becoming a Humor Being,* (Lindenhurst, Full Circle Publishing, 2000)

- David Glickman, *"But I'm Not Funny!"—76 Ways to Get Any Audience Laughing Anytime, Anywhere,* (Brandon, October Publishing, 2002)

- *Les Miserables (1987 Original Broadway Cast),* (Decca US, 1990)

- *Man of La Mancha (Original 1965 Broadway Cast),* (Decca US, 2001)

- *Come Away with Me,* Nora Jones, (Blue Note Records, 2002)

- *The Hallelujah Chorus,* George Frideric Handel, London Philharmonic Choir and Orchestra, (Sparrow Emd, 2002)

- Harry L. Woodward, Mark J. Tager, *Leadership in Times of Stress and Change—Seven Skills for Gaining Trust and Inspiring Confidence,* (La Jolla, WorkSkills-LifeSkills, 2002)

- Dr. Suess, *Horton Hears a Who,* (New York, Random House, 1954)

- Don W. Larson, *Land of the Giants—A History of Minnesota Business,* (Minneapolis, Dorn Books, 1979)

- John P. Schuster, *Answering Your Call—A Guide for Living Your Deepest Purpose,* (San Francisco, Berrett-Koehler Publishers, 2003)

- Richard J. Leider, *The Power of Purpose—Creating Meaning in Your Life and Work,* (New York, MJF Books, 1997)

- Mihaly Csikszentmihalyi, *Finding Flow—The Psychology of Engagement with Everyday Life,* (New York, Basic Books, 1997)

- John Izzo, *Second Innocence—Rediscovering joy and wonder,* (San Francisco, Berrett-Koehler Publishers, 2004)

ABOUT
THE AUTHOR

John M. Bean

A Hudson Institute-certified personal, executive, and team coach, John Bean specializes in the power of renewal through purpose, vision, and values. John brings over 30 years of business experience to a wide variety of organizations and associations.

John is a well-respected, popular, and dynamic keynote speaker. His distinctive style energizes, educates, and entertains his audiences. He moves his audience and readers with his unique blend of business, performing, and life experiences. Among the organizations who have heard him are American Express, Amherst College, Boeing Leadership Center, The Washington Initiative Employment Conference, Minneapolis College of Art and Design, Minnesota Department of Health, The Stanton Group, Care Providers of Minnesota, South Central Minnesota Nursing Home Social Work Association, Midwest Pension Conference, and Hudson Institute of Santa Barbara.

A confidential consultant and advisor to business leaders of all kinds, John says, "I have been in the relationship business for 30 years as an investment advisor, personal coach, professional speaker, and volunteer. My mission is a simple one: To help people get where they want to go by lighting the way through coaching, speaking, and consulting, mixed with a bit of humor and gentle whimsy.

"Work," he says, "whether it is the work of an organization or a family, doesn't have to be a grim battle. If we recognize the contributions each of us has the potential to make and if we encourage and nourish each other's unique gifts, we can attain not only our financial goals, but our fulfillment as human beings. The two are not, nor should they be, mutually exclusive."

John has been a board member, contributor, and fundraiser for several community service organizations including the Minnesota Children's Museum (founding board member), Washburn Child Guidance Center, American Red Cross, Minnesota Dance Theater, and American Cancer Society.

As a former singer and entertainer John has appeared on stages from LA to Washington, D.C., Mexico, and the Virgin Islands. He served on active duty in the U.S. Army, with a Top Secret security clearance (1970–72).

He holds a bachelor of arts degree in dramatic arts from Amherst College in Amherst, Massachusetts. He is a guest lecturer at the University of St. Thomas in St. Paul, Minnesota.

John currently lives in the Twin Cities where he enjoys life with his wonderful wife of more than 30 years. He adores his two children and three grandchildren.

If you would like John to be a keynote speaker, or to host a workshop, you can contact him at 612-387-4510, e-mail at *john@johnmbean.com*, or visit his Web site at *www.johnmbean. com.*

ORDERING INFORMATION
To purchase additional copies of
PhB: The Professional Human Being
Go to *www.BookHouseFulfillment.com*
Or call 1-800-901-3480
Reseller discounts available.